ISLANDS OF SOUTHERN
LAKE WINNIPESAUKEE

ISLANDS OF SOUTHERN
LAKE WINNIPESAUKEE

STEPHANIE A. ERICKSON

THE
History
PRESS

Published by The History Press
Charleston, SC
www.historypress.com

Back cover image: Southern Lake Winnipesaukee from the summit of Mount Major, Alton, New Hampshire. *iStock photo by kadecanessa.*

First published 2024

Manufactured in the United States

ISBN 9781467155465

Library of Congress Control Number: 2024930895

CONTENTS

Acknowledgments   9
Introduction   11

Geology of the Islands   15
Indigenous History   23
The Mason Grant   27
Sleepers Island   33
Rattlesnake Island   55
Diamond Island   65
Treasure Island and Cub Island   75
Ship Island and Moose Island   95
The Islands of Alton Bay and East Alton   97
The Barndoor Islands   103
Parker Island   111
Worcester Island   115
The Varney Islands   117

Bibliography   135
Index   139
About the Author   143

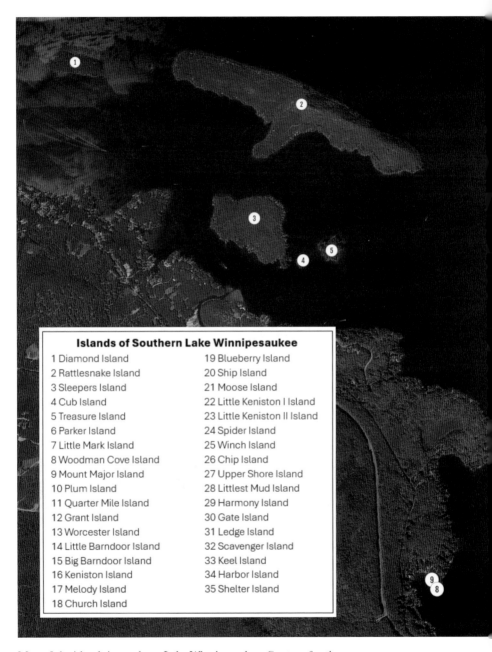

Islands of Southern Lake Winnipesaukee

1 Diamond Island
2 Rattlesnake Island
3 Sleepers Island
4 Cub Island
5 Treasure Island
6 Parker Island
7 Little Mark Island
8 Woodman Cove Island
9 Mount Major Island
10 Plum Island
11 Quarter Mile Island
12 Grant Island
13 Worcester Island
14 Little Barndoor Island
15 Big Barndoor Island
16 Keniston Island
17 Melody Island
18 Church Island

19 Blueberry Island
20 Ship Island
21 Moose Island
22 Little Keniston I Island
23 Little Keniston II Island
24 Spider Island
25 Winch Island
26 Chip Island
27 Upper Shore Island
28 Littlest Mud Island
29 Harmony Island
30 Gate Island
31 Ledge Island
32 Scavenger Island
33 Keel Island
34 Harbor Island
35 Shelter Island

Map of the islands in southern Lake Winnipesaukee. *Courtesy of author.*

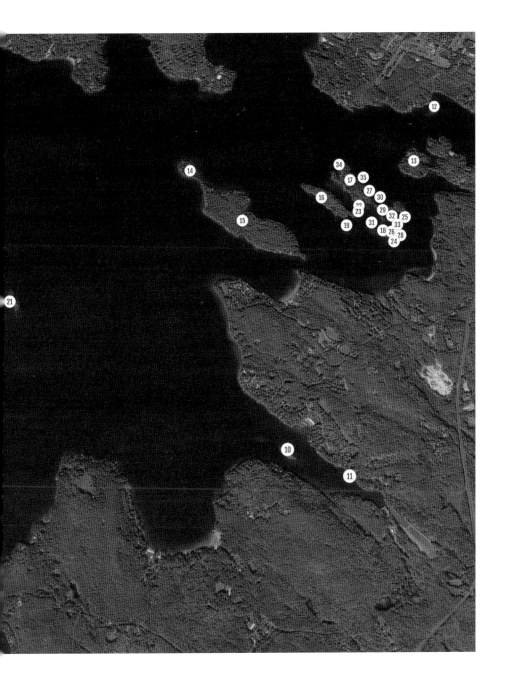

ACKNOWLEDGMENTS

S pecial thanks to the individuals and the individuals, towns and historical societies for their contributions to this publication:

New Hampshire State Library, Concord; Library of Congress; New Hampshire Historical Society, Concord; University of New Hampshire Diamond Library, Milne Special Collections, Durham; Library of Congress Archives; Judson D. Hale and family; John D. Spooner; Rick Nash; Evan Walsh; Richard Boisvert of the New Hampshire Archaeological Society; Lake Winnipesaukee Historical Society, Laconia, New Hampshire; Mr. Gene Denu, archivist for the Wolfeboro Historical Society, Wolfeboro, New Hampshire; Robert J. Girouard; the Mercier family; L. Sanders Cutter; the Girl Scout Museum at Cedar Hill, Waltham, Massachusetts; and members of the Winnipesaukee forum for their wealth of random knowledge of the lake and islands.

INTRODUCTION

My husband and I purchased property on Sleepers Island in 2015. Our property contained a small cabin that, after research, was found to be the former sales office for the Deer Haven Development Corporation when the island was divested in the mid-1960s. As we were cleaning out the cabin for renovation, we uncovered the original sales and advertising documents from the development corporation. As an avid researcher, I wanted to learn more, and that thirst for information became an obsession to learn everything about "our island" and the original residents who built the island castle and lie at rest in the island cemetery.

As my family's historian, I knew that I had the Sleeper surname in a maternal line. When we purchased our camp property, I didn't even make the connection between my Sleeper line and the island. We came to find out that Nehemiah Sleeper, the original Sleeper of New Durham Gore (Alton) and Sleepers Island, is my sixth great-grandfather. Once that connection was made, I felt compelled to continue my research into the history of Sleepers Island. As my quest for more information became an obsession, researching this book took on a life of its own. I spent hours going down all manner of rabbit holes to pull snippets of information out about Sleepers Island and the surrounding islands in the southern half of Lake Winnipesaukee. I spent days upon days researching online, reading family histories and scouring old newspapers for a mention of the island and its colonial settlers. This book is the culmination of four years of that research.

Major Otis Grant Hammond, a former director of the New Hampshire Historical Society (1913–44), found 132 forms of the spelling of the lake name—including "Winnipiscokee," "Winepesocky," "Winepiseoka," "Winniepeseocke" and "Nikisipsque"—in old documents, maps and historical writings. His report displayed the need for uniform spelling, and a legislative act in 1933 did just that. In 1933, the State of New Hampshire made the legal spelling of the lake "Winnipesaukee." Bizer Corporation lists 253 islands on Lake Winnipesaukee. There is some discrepancy in this number, as some sources claim 274 and others 365, one for each day of the year. What defines an island in Winnipesaukee is flexible and vague. Encyclopedia Britannica will tell you that an island is any area of land smaller than a continent that is entirely surrounded by water. Islands can occur in any body of water from oceans to lakes and even in rivers. A group of islands is called an archipelago. In Lake Winnipesaukee, the islands range from dense forested tracts of land with summits that provide 360-degree views of the lake to piles of boulders dropped by the glaciers. The largest island in the lake is Long Island at 1,186 acres and is located in the town of Moultonborough. It is bridged with the mainland shore. The smallest island in the lake with a "structure" is Becky's Garden in Center Harbor. Several of the named Varney Islands challenge Becky's "smallest island" title.

There are forty-five named islands in the southern half of the lake. Alton has eleven named islands: Rattlesnake, Sleepers, Treasure, Cub, Barndoor, Ship, Moose, Little Mark, Woodman Cove, Mount Major Island and Plum Islands. Wolfeboro contains the majority of islands in this section of the lake at thirty-three, most of which are located in the region of the Varney Islands. However, many of the Wolfeboro islands are unoccupied, unbuildable or so low in elevation that they cannot be found in times of high water. Gilford has approximately twenty-two islands, but only Diamond Islands is located in this area of the lake. The majority of the islands on the lake lie within or at the entrances of harbors and coves.

The islands of Winnipesaukee are unique. Some share a common history, and other histories are affected by the culture of the town or area of the lake. The histories are the result of the indigenous culture of the land, the colonial settlers of the area and the summer vacationers traveling to grasp a piece of the Winnipesaukee spirit. Many of our islands contain unique ecosystems or flora and fauna. Darwin's theory of evolution may not have been developed without his exploration and observation of island biodiversity. Living on an island is not without its challenges. Any islander will tell you a story of the challenges of building, maintenance and repair of their island camp; of the fierce northwest wind that can blow; or of falling in the lake while moving furniture, lumber or other items from the dock to the boat or from the boat to the cottage. Islanders are resilient and resourceful and always willing to help one another. Each island forms its own miniature community ecosystem among the residents and the deer, moose and bear that swim to the islands to share in isolation.

GEOLOGY OF THE ISLANDS

The bedrock geology of the area occurred in three major ages. About 380 million years ago, a shallow sea covered most of New England. Small marine animals left shells that accumulated and buried over tens of millions of years. In time, these layers of shells, coral, calcareous algae and plankton hardened into shales, sandstones and limestones. This first sedimentary rock formation is called the Littleton Formation. The accumulation of sedimentary rock was interrupted by a deformation in Earth's crust that folded the sedimentary beds into steep dipping layers. Heat and pressure increased, and the minerals of mica and garnet were formed. The shales, sandstones and limestones became schist, quartzite and gneiss.

Lake Winnipesaukee is surrounded by four igneous-volcanic complexes. These volcanic complexes formed during the Mesozoic era, likely during the breakup of the supercontinent Pangea. The islands in Southern Lake Winnipesaukee are located within the Belknap Mountain Complex, and the intrusive rocks here date to 169 to 150 million years old. Rattlesnake Island, Diamond Island, Ship and Moose are part of the Belknap Ring Fracture Intrusion and represent the edges of an extinct volcanic caldera. The Belknap Mountain Complex intrudes through the Winnipesaukee Tonalite, which is included in the New Hampshire Plutonic Series, indicating that the Winnipesaukee Tonalite is the parent rock in the region. Sleepers Island, the Wolfeboro Islands and the Islands of Alton Bay are underlain by the Winnipesaukee Tonalite and Quartz Diorite, consisting of a gray, massive to foliated tonalite and minor quartz diorite, granodiorite and granite.

Several unique geological formations can be observed diving off the shores of Parker Island and off the shores of Clark's Point in Wolfeboro. Glacial striations can be observed on the underwater shelf, and a large quartz vein has been exposed. The ledge forms what looks like a giant staircase that extends from about twenty feet from the shoreline to approximately forty feet from the shoreline. It is estimated that more than two thousand linear miles of ice moved over the bedrock ledges of the Winnipesaukee area. The glacial ice was vertically at least one mile thick. The bedrock on the top of Mount Washington indicates that the glacier moved over the peak. As the glacier advanced, it dragged with it all the weathered and eroded fragments, creating an abrasive sandpaper for the rocks below.

Lake Winnipesaukee and the islands within it were formed during the retreat of the Wisconsinian Ice Age, our last ice age, about fourteen thousand years ago. Winnipesaukee formed in an area of deep glacial erosion. Based on information from area geologic investigations, prior to this ice age, no lake existed in this location. As the glacial ice receded north, fragments of weathered bedrock were pulled off the bedrock, forming the islands of Winnipesaukee and the area mountains. The glacial ice scoured the area under Lake Winnipesaukee, forming the lake base, and glacial meltwaters filled the basin. North of Rattlesnake Island, between Diamond Island and Welch Island, lies the deepest waters in Lake Winnipesaukee at 213 feet. Deep, cold-water fish species such as the cusk and salmon can often be found in this area.

The orientation of Lake Winnipesaukee from northwest to southeast is the result of the direction of the glaciers. All the glacial striations are oriented in this direction.

According to the U.S. Department of Agriculture, Soil Survey for Belknap County, the soils on the islands are classified as Tunbridge-Lyman-Becket (TNB) complex, with slopes ranging from 8 to 60 percent. TNB soils are derived from a basal meltout till with a parent material of granite, gneiss or schist. The depth to bedrock is shallow on the islands, with depths as shallow as ten to twenty inches. The topography we see today was greatly shaped by the glacial accretion and retreat of the last continental glaciation. Glaciation was followed by a reworking of the surface by wind and water erosion.

The surface of the islands is riddled with glacial erratic boulders, remnants of the glacier's retreat during the last ice age. A glacial erratic is a rock that has been transported by ice and deposited in an area not native to its formation. The glacial erratics in the Winnipesaukee region are primarily composed of the Winnipesaukee Tonalite or the Conway Granite. These boulders could have been carried by the ice as few as a few feet to as far as twenty-five miles. The fine sand and silt that would have surrounded the boulders eroded over time and were transported into the sandbars around the lake. The boulders are more concentrated where wave action is high. Some of the islands of the lake such as Governors Island and Long Island are connected by boulder spits. These spits formed harbors for small craft. The longest boulder spit in Lake Winnipesaukee is more than five hundred feet long and connects Black Island to Moultonborough Neck. Shorter spits can be observed in and around the Varney Islands and form some of the smaller Varneys.

Lake Winnipesauke once flowed in the opposite direction toward the southeast down Alton Bay and through the Merrymeeting River toward the Atlantic Ocean. The Glacial Lake New Durham drained most of the Winnipesaukee Basin until the glacier terminus receded to the north of Gilford, New Hampshire, damming the outflow with glacial debris. Once this occurred, the Winnipesaukee Basin was able to drain toward the west, as it does today, through Paugus Bay into the Winnipesaukee River. As the glacier retreated, New England was left with many glacial lakes, Lake Winnipesaukee being one result. As the lake began to drain, the Winnipesaukee River

Sleepers Island shoreline showing glacial boulders and glacial erratics, 2019. *Photo by author.*

was formed and began to cut channels into the same glacial sediment left behind in the glacier's wake. No vegetation would have been present, so the landscape was reworked and shaped through erosion. Just as with the ice that forms each year and redistributes the docks on the lake, the winter ice would have continued to erode and reshape the landscape. Frost in the ground would have raised and tilled the glacial boulders to the surface. The sandbars of Small's Cove, Braun Bay and Timber Island formed as the waters of the lake worked the sand grains trapped between boulders, and then waves move the sand grains back and forth until they reached the closest head of a bay or channel.

After the retreat, trees would have been few and far between, and New Hampshire would have looked similar in terrain to the tundra in northern Canada. Studies of pollen, cones and stems in swamps and bogs tell us that between fourteen thousand and nine thousand years ago, New Hampshire was a tundra-like biome, with arctic plants and sedge grasses. Vegetation would have been primarily mosses and lichen, sedge grasses willows and dwarf birches. Conifers such as fir, spruce and pine would have followed.

The climate thirteen thousand years ago would have been reflected in cooler and wetter summers similar to interior Labrador, Canada. The climate became drier and drier as the glaciers continued to retreat north. Pollen evidence indicates that there were strong climatic fluctuations.

Lake Winnipesaukee is the largest lake in the state of New Hampshire and the third-largest lake in New England behind Lake Champlain in Vermont and Moosehead Lake in Maine. The elevation of Lake Winnipesaukee is currently 505 feet above mean sea level (msl). This elevation is now controlled by the spillway at the Lakeport Dam in Laconia.

FLORA AND FAUNA

The islands contain many native species of plants. Indigenous groups forged on the islands of Winnipesaukee. In the mid-1850s, the islands of Winnipesaukee became known for their berries, such as blueberries (both high and low bush) and huckleberries. Locals and tourists would row over to the islands to have a picnic and pick the berries for pies and jams. A 2011 report indicated that Rattlesnake Island has 255 different native and nonnative (introduced after 1901) plant species. The dominant species on the islands are trees.

Huckleberries (*Gaylussacia baccata*) are native to many of the islands. They are also called "whortleberries" at times, which is the English name of a group of fruiting bushes that include huckleberries, berries and other similar fruits. Huckleberries are found along the shoreline of the island in bushes containing small black or red berries, in the same habitats that support blueberries. The underside of the huckleberry leaf features resin dots that will glitter in the sun. They are tarter than a blueberry but can be used interchangeably in recipes.

Black tupelo (*Nyssa sylvatica*) trees dot the shorelines of the island. Tupelos are identified by their glossy green leaves and alligator-like bark. In the fall, the tree produces greenish white flowers and bluish black fruits. They are some of the brightest trees on the shoreline during fall foliage, turning bright orange, bright red, yellow or purple shades. Tupelo trees are an important winter food source for birds and deer, and its flowers are prized for their nectar. Birds will feed on the winter berries on the tree, and deer graze on the sweet twigs of the tree. The black berries are edible and have a sour taste. They can be used to make jelly, jams and juice or used in baking recipes. Honey from the black tupelo has a light and mild taste.

White pine (*Pinus strobus*) was a premier wood that was sought after by logging and timber companies around the lake in the 1800s. Indigenous peoples combined pine pitch with charcoal and bear grease to provide waterproofing for their boats. The white pines on the islands of Winnipesaukee were used to construct many of the early structures and residences around the lake. By the turn of the twentieth century, many of the islands had been deforested of their white pine. The hurricane of 1938 took out many of the remaining white pines on the island. Sleepers Island now contains many stands of white pines, although they are not as prevalent a species on the islands as they were one hundred years ago. The dominant tree species is now the eastern hemlock.

The eastern hemlock (*Tsuga canadensis*) is a slow-growing coniferous tree. It is identified by its needles, which grow in a flat pattern low on the branches of the tree. In recent years, with temperatures increasing in the region, the eastern hemlock has been attacked by the hemlock wooly adelgid, an aphid that feed exclusively on hemlock.

Ironwood (*Betulaceae ostryain*) trees are small, understory trees that have the ability to grow in almost any location. It is a member of the birch family and shares many characteristics with birch and elm trees, although ironwood is often significantly smaller. Ironwood can be identified by its hop-like fruit and clusters of papery, seed-bearing pods that grow between one inch and two inches long. Ironwood exhibits slow growth, and as such, it forms strong timber. It is one of the hardest of all the native North American tree species. The wood of the ironwood tree is used for making tool handles, fence posts and mallets.

Several species of maple trees exist on the island, including red maple (*Acer rubrum*) and sugar maple (*Acer saccharum*). Maple trees are an important source of maple sap for the production of maple syrup.

White oak (*Quercus alba*) has also been a primary timber product that was sourced from the islands. Many of the original homes in Alton and Wolfeboro were built from white oak from the islands of the lake. Thomas Flanders built the first decked boat on Winnipesaukee, the *Rockingham*, using white oak sourced from the islands. It is possible that he sourced his white oak for both the *Rockingham* and his home in Alton from Sleepers Island based on the island's former name of Flanders Island.

Birch trees (*Betula papyrifera* and *Betula alleghaniensis*) are another prevalent deciduous tree on the island. Indigenous people constructed birch-bark canoes using the bark from the trees to wrap their watercraft. Chaga, a fungus that grows on the trunks of birch trees, was used to make medicinal tea.

Many species of birds and mammals can be found on the island. Loons, mergansers, mallard ducks, gray herons and bald eagles are among the frequent birds seen in and around the island waters. Several families of deer are frequent foragers of planted and native flowers around the island. Deer can often be seen swimming between the shores of Sleepers, Cub and Treasure Islands and between the islands and the mainland.

Wild turkeys are frequent visitors on the island recreation trails, and many families of mink can be seen making their homes along the rocky shorelines. Raccoons are rarely found but have been recently spotted again on the islands, foraging through summer residents' refuse. Additionally, several species of squirrels, small rodents and a fisher cat have been reported by island residents. Black bears have been reported as visitors to the islands but typically do not make the island their homes. Bears, like the deer and moose of the area, swim between the islands and the mainland foraging for food.

The flora and fauna of Lake Winnipesaukee have long been inspiration for writers and artists. Marian Longfellow, the niece of the poet Henry Wadsworth Longfellow, was inspired by the natural beauty of the lake when she captured the twilight hours on the lake in her 1904 poem "Lake Winnepesogee":

(T<small>WILIGHT</small>)
O fair, broad Lake, upon whose breast
The Shifting shadows rise and fall.
Thy surging waters' vague unrest
Sinks beneath twilight's gathering pall.

Thy changing beauties quickly glide
Successive past th' entranced eye,
While hills around, in regal pride,
Reflected in thy waters lie.

I hear the plash or dipping oar,
I see boats swing on their way;
The waves flow on from shore to shore,
While Softly, slowly dies the sky.

And sweetly with the evening's calm
Upon my heart there falls a peace,
That comes as come the evening psalm,
That bids the world's vain tumult cease.

And as fall swift the shades of night
Along thy path my feet must tread,
Lo I through the clouds a golden light
Upon life's passing scene is shed.

And so, bathed in its softened glow,
And tuned to sweetest harmonies
Far, far beyond Life's ebb and flow—
The soul, immortal, seeks the skies!

INDIGENOUS HISTORY

Lake Winnipesaukee (*Wiwininebesake*) and its islands were originally occupied by the indigenous groups of the Algonquins. "Abenaki" has been a name applied to Algonquin tribes in northern New England. The Abenaki group occupied the majority of the lands of New England and Canada to the St. Lawrence River. They called this territory *N' Dakinna* or "My Homelands." The Abenaki word *WiWininebesake* has been translated to mean "beautiful water in a high place" or "the Smile of the Great Spirit," depending on whose translation you use. Finds at the Aquadoctan site (The Weirs) indicate that the Abenakis occupied this area of Lake Winnipesaukee since at least 7600 BCE. The Eastern Abenakis occupied the lands primarily in Maine, and the Western Abenakis occupied the lands of New Hampshire and Vermont.

Archaeological evidence indicates that the earliest human inhabitants in the Northeast date to approximately ten thousand years ago. These earliest humans would have primarily been big game hunters. They would have hunted giant mammoths, mastodons, dire wolves, saber-tooth tigers and giant beavers in addition to the common elk, caribou and moose of today.

Archaeological evidence from the Paleo-Indian period (11,000 to 9,000 years ago) indicates that the Algonquin settlements were focused on waterways, streams, lakes, rivers and wetlands. Many of the archaeological sites in New Hampshire have been found along the shores of our waterways, indicating that the water was extremely important in their transportation, food and trading. As the large game began to go extinct, the people who remained would have turned to other sources of food such as gathering herbs, wild vegetables, fish and smaller game. The diversity of resources in these areas was necessary for a nomadic lifestyle. Radiocarbon dating from The Weirs site indicate that it was occupied 9,615 (+/-225) years before present by a nomadic population that would have relied on hunting for sustenance and fashioned tools using various sources that were not always local.

Today, all the indigenous tribes of the area are classified as Algonquin. The Algonquian Confederacy is a large family that consists of more than twenty languages. "Abenaki" applies to members of the Algonquian Confederacy in northern New England; the Abenakis and further designated Eastern Abenakis, those primarily in the areas of what is now Maine; and the Western Abenakis, those primarily in the areas that are now Vermont and New Hampshire. The Abenaki tribes of the Penacook, Ossipee and Winnipesaukee occupied New Hampshire lands surrounding Winnipesaukee from about thirteen thousand years ago until the Battle of Cocheco (1676). Mainland areas in Alton including Camp Kabeyun at Clay Point and Roberts Cove were known Abenaki camping grounds. Alton Bay was the location of the Abenaki village Quannippi, translated as "long water." The Quannippi trail begins at "the place where the water flows out of the pond," Win-nebos-e-kek (Rust Pond, Wolfeboro), and followed the eastern shore of Lake Winnipesaukee to Clay Point and Fort Point. The Ossipee tribe of the Sokoki Nation occupied the lands of the northeast portion (Wolfeboro area) of the lake. The southwest area of the lake was land occupied by tribes of the Penacook Confederacy. The two nations would meet on a small island south of Moultonboro Neck to conduct trade.

The Abenaki traveled the lake in *woleskaolakws*, or hollowed-out boats. The bases of trees would be slowly burned until it was felled, and then slow fires were set to hollow out the log into a canoe. The flora on the islands provided materials for life on the lake. Pine pitch from the white pines would be added to charcoal and bear grease to waterproof the canoe. Chaga on birch trees around the lake was used to make medicinal teas. Berries that grow in abundance on the islands would be a source of food and antioxidants. Rattlesnake plantain, a woodland orchid, was previously found on Rattlesnake Island in abundance. Rattlesnake plantain is now typically only found in the western United States and throughout Canada. The Abenakis believed that this plant was an antidote for snakebites. The roots of the plant would have been made into a teas to treat lung inflammations as well. The leaves would have been used to calm an upset stomach, as a cold treatment or for joint or tooth aches. The wilted leaves would have been used similar to aloe to cool burns, reduce inflammation of skin lesions or as a pain reliever.

The Abenaki population was tragically depleted with the "Indian Fever" epidemic of 1616–19. It is estimated that more than 90 percent of the Abenaki population was wiped out during this epidemic. The epidemic was described as a pestilential putrid fever. Those afflicted were described as having jaundice and hemorrhaging from the nose. Scientists suspect that this epidemic was either chicken pox, smallpox or hepatic fever, all diseases that would have been transmitted through contact with the colonial settlers. After epidemics and the Cochecho Massacre, the majority of the remaining tribes fled north toward Canada, only returning to the lake for hunting and fishing expeditions.

THE MASON GRANT

In 1620, King Charles I created a council of forty "noblemen, knights, and gentlemen, by the name of the Council established at Plymouth, in the county of Devon for the Planting, Ruling and Governing of New England in America: from the fortieth to the forty-eighth-north latitude." Captain John Mason and Sir Fernando Gorges were the two most active in the Council. For their service, King Charles granted land in the new colonies to the pair. Captain Mason was charged with providing military and civil tasks along the newly established New England coast between 1620 and 1622. Captain Mason succeeded in his tasks of thwarting pirates, protecting fishing and adding to navigation and chart knowledge of the North Atlantic coast. As a result of his success, Captain Mason was awarded three land grants from the king. The "Mason Grant," as it became known by colonists, was land that comprises Maine, New Hampshire and Massachusetts today. Mason was awarded all the lands between the Merrimack River and the Sagadock (Kennebec) River and north to the St. Lawrence River. Gorges and Mason formed a partnership with New England merchants and began to create settlements along the Piscataquog River. At Captain Mason's death in 1635, the Masonian lands passed down through Captain John Mason's heirs, his wife and son Joseph Mason.

By 1641, the expenses on the lands had begun to outweigh the income, and Mason's wife and heirs began to sell off tracts of land, some of which fell under the jurisdiction of the Massachusetts Bay Colony and, subsequently, the grandsons of John Tufton and Robert Tufton. The grandsons were required to take the surname Mason as part of the land deed transfer. The Massachusetts Bay Colonies began issuing town charters in what would become New Hampshire until 1679. In 1679, New Hampshire became a "royal province," although Massachusetts continued to claim the Merrimack Valley for another six decades.

Massachusetts and New Hampshire waged several legal battles with the Crown of England over who held jurisdiction over the Mason Grant. In the end, the Mason heirs and their agent, John Thomlinson, won out. Benning Wentworth was appointed governor of the Province of New Hampshire in 1741 by King George II. Benning began expanding New Hampshire borders through land grants and military commissions. It was often said that he turned a blind eye to the White Pine Laws, appeasing the timber industry by allowing merchants free access to New Hampshire white pine forests as long as they continued to supply masts to his brother Mark, who sold them to the British navy. In 1708, the New Hampshire General Court enacted a law to protect and preserve all trees for the British navy so long as they were a certain size. Sawmills found processing these trees were fined fifty pounds for each illegally harvested tree because they were in a sense owned by the Crown under this 1706 law.

Thomlinson in 1746 conveyed his interest in the lands of New Hampshire to Theodore Atkinson (brother-in-law to Governor Benning Wentworth), John Wentworth, Mark Hunting Wentworth, George Jaffrey, Richard Wibird, Samuel Moore, Nathaniel Meserve, Thomas Packer, Thomas Wallingford, Jonathan Ordione, Joshua Pierce and John Moffat for £1,500. Atkinson had three shares, Mark Hunting Wentworth two shares and the other ten one share each. These twelve individuals in Portsmouth became known as the Masonian Proprietors. The proprietors were responsible for the original township grants as New Hampshire was incorporated as a state.

The Masonian Proprietors were all related in some manner to the Wentworth family. Mark Hunting Wentworth and John Wentworth were brothers. They were the sons of Lieutenant Governor John Wentworth and brother of Governor Benning Wentworth. Mark Hunting Wentworth was the father of Governor John Wentworth of the Wentworth estate in Wolfeboro. John succeeded Benning as governor of New Hamphire. Theodore Atkinson married his first cousin, Frances Deering Wentworth, who was also the cousin of John Wentworth and the niece of Benning and Mark Hunking Wenworth. Frances later scandalously married her cousin John Wentworth, just two weeks after the death of her first husband, Theodore, and just before John became the last royal governor of New

Hampshire. Thomas Packer married Rebecca Wentworth, the sister of Benning and Mark Hunking Wentworth. His second wife was the mother of John Rindge and sister to Jotham Ordiorne Sr. John Rindge was the brother-in-law to Mark Hunting Wentworth. George Jaffrey was Mark Hunting and John Wentworth's nephew. Richard Wibird's sister married another Wentworth brother. Joshua and Daniel Pierce were brothers. Daniel married Ann Rindge, sister of John Rindge. Samuel Moore was a colonel in the New Hampshire regiment at Louisberg and married a sister of the Pierce brothers. Clement March was related to the Pierce family as well. John Moffatt and Thomas Wallingford were the only two proprietors not related by marriage or blood to the Wentworth family. However, the Moffatts were still a prominent Portsmouth family.

Colonel Blanchard and his son were hired to survey the inland limits of the Mason property. The land boundaries were interpreted on a sixty-mile radius from the mouth of each river. A curve was drawn on the map, and the boundaries of the lands were set. Meanwhile, the proprietors conveyed townships to themselves and to other groups of organized land developers. Goffstown was the first town granted by the proprietors in 1748. For the following forty years, the Masonian proprietors were responsible for the granting of all towns in New Hampshire. They granted thirty-seven townships in New Hampshire, including New Durham Gore (Alton) and Wolfeboro. Towns were created as squares within the map, with each side being approximately six miles wide, as was established by the Public Land Survey System in 1785. Leftover areas in between the township squares and the sixty-mile radius boundary became free-style irregular boundaries.

In 1759, one of those six-by-six-mile township squares was created for the lands northeast of "Winnepesoky Pond." Thirty-six square miles were granted to Henry Athorp, Ammi Ruhamah Cutter, David Sewall and William Treadwell. The area was broken up into four parcels, giving each family about one thousand acres apiece and a bounty not to exceed £250 sterling. The four men worked on advertising the area as prime farmland, but it was years before the first permanent settlement was established in the area. Benjamin Blake built a log cabin on what is now North Main Street in 1768. William Fullerton, Joseph Lary, James Lucas, Thomas Taylor, Thomas Pipe and Samuel Tibbetts soon followed Blake. These seven men would be the original founding families of what would become known as Wolfeboro. Reuben Libby and Henry Rust followed in 1771. John Wentworth had been appointment by King George II as governor of the state and surveyors of the Kings Woods in North America. He began to build his estate in the

Kings Woods in 1766. New Hampshire's lands were still part of the British colony, and its tall white pine trees were reserved for use as ship masts for the Royal Navy. As these trees were in the Kings Woods, the area became known as Kingswood.

There were sixty original proprietors of Kingswood in the Province of New Hampshire. These include members of the Rogers, Parker and Pierce families and some of the Masonian proprietors who would be integral in the history of the towns surrounding the lake and the history of the islands themselves. The conditions of the grant from Governor Belcher saw each build a dwelling house and settle a family within five years. They also were instructed to build a meetinghouse, settle an orthodox minister, reserve three hundred acres for the first ordained minister to settle in the town and reserve an additional six hundred acres for parsonages and three hundred acres for schools. The sixty proprietors were required to pay a rent of ten pounds of hemp and reserve all mast trees. In a meeting in 1759 in Portsmouth, it was voted that "the township, in honor of the late renowned General Wolfe, deceased, be called Wolf-borough." General James Wolfe was a British army officer associated with the military expeditions of the East Coast and was a popular officer. He was killed in a battle with the French at the Plains of Abraham in Quebec on September 13, 1759, during the Seven Years' War. There was an error in the spelling of General Wolfe's name in the town charter, and it took a century for the name to become standardized to the current spelling of Wolfeboro. The spelling was made official in 1907 by the state legislature.

By 1760, the Masonian Proprietors had begun selling off pieces of the grant to individuals to form towns. Gilmanton was the first town on the lake to be settled by colonists. Town growth was slow until after the Revolutionary War, when it rapidly increased and soon surrounded the whole lake. Gilmanton was named after the Gilman family, who comprised twenty-four of the original settlers in the area. As population increased, the islands of Winnipesaukee became sources of the white pine for construction of homes and boats. The Masonian Proprietors quickly began dividing up settlements into two-hundred- to four-hundred-acre lots to entice colonists to settle in the new towns around the lake.

The Masonian proprietors met in Portsmouth on December 24, 1781, to formally divide the unallotted territory in the Winnipesaukee lakes region. The plan that was submitted at the meeting called "Draft of the Islands in Winipiseokee Pond, as numbered and coupled in the first plan." All of the original grantees of the islands were members of a new company that acquired the remaining rights of the old Mason Grant. These names appear with land allotments in every town granted by the company.

The islands of Winnipesaukee were divided up and allotted to fifteen "Masonian proprietors." The larger islands were split between two or more proprietors, while the smaller islands were grouped together in lots. Sleepers Island, then known as Flanders Island, was included in Lot No. 1, along with a group of four islands near Wolfeboro called "Barndoor Islands," the easterly end of Rattlesnake Island and Diamond Island. Lot No. 1 was granted to John Tufton Mason and John Tomlinson. The western half of Rattlesnake was included in Lot No. 2, granted to Mark Hunting Wentworth. The islands of Alton Bay, Ship Island, Moose Island, Varney Islands and Parker Island are included in the un-numbered islands in a later transaction.

TABLE: ALLOCATION OF THE NUMBERED ISLANDS

Lot No.	Masonian Proprietor(s)	Island
1	John Thomlinson and John Tufton Mason	East Rattlesnake, Barndoor Islands (Barndoor, Little Barndoor, Keniston, Melody), Sleepers, Diamond
2	Mark Hunting Wentworth	West Rattlesnake
3	Samuel Solly and Clement March	Welch
4	Thomas Wallingford	Long Island, Five Mile, Six Mile
5	Richard Wibird	Long Island
6	Nathaniel Meserve, Joseph Blanchard, Joseph Green and Paul March	Long Island
7	Daniel Peirce	Long Island
8	George Jaffrey	Long Island
9	John Rindge	Jolly, Birch, Steamboat, Round, Lockes, Mark
10	Thomas Packer	South Bear
11	Theodore Atkinson	North Bear plus part of Small Bear

12	Jotham Odiorne	Pine, Stonedam
13	John Wentworth	Three Mile, Big Beaver, Blackcat, Hull, Blueberry, Pitchwood, Nine Acre, Whortleberry, Sandy, Dow, Chases, Farm
14	Mary Moore (widow of Colonel Samuel Moore)	North Cow, Little Bear, Timber
15	John Moffatt	South Cow

The first plan of Winnipesaukee was drafted between 1766 and 1770. A survey of the lake was completed by James Hersey in 1772 and first identifies Sleepers Island as "Flanders Island," referring to the Flanders family, some of the original settlers of New Durham Gore (incorporated as Alton in 1796). Hersey estimated the island's size as seventy-nine acres. Rattlesnake Island, Barndoor Islands and Diamond Island have no previously known names and presumably have been named the same since the time of the Masonian grants. Approximately 235 islands were included in the unnumbered islands. These islands were owned jointly by default by all the Masonian Proprietors. As an original proprietor died, the land and islands passed on to their heirs. The islands and surrounding areas were coveted for their natural assets, fur-bearing animals, fish and trees (lumber/masts).

SLEEPERS ISLAND

It will be early on a calm, warm late June morning on New Hampshire's Lake Winnipesaukee. I'll walk down to the water's edge below my camp on Sleepers Island, rest on the bench I built there years before, and sip from a mug of hot coffee. The sun will glisten through the tall pine trees behind me. From the distance, I'll hear the faint sound of an outboard motor, but the huge lake before me, lying there in its myriad of undulating reflections, will be otherwise free of human activity. Then, far down near the Witches and Forty Islands, I'll see a dark, faintly ominous looking band of ruffled water creeping slowly toward me along the entire breadth of the lake from Meredith Bay to Moultonborough Neck. There will be long-ago voices and laughter like distant music. A solitary leaf on the poplar tree leaning over the shore near me will flap lazily as if in preparation for the daily summertime wind-inevitably on its way always.
—Judson Hale, 1982

Sleepers Island, a parcel of land containing about 110 acres, is located in Alton, Belknap County, New Hampshire, lying between the westerly shore of Lake Winnipesaukee and Rattlesnake Island to the northward. Sleepers Island rises approximately 696 feet above sea level at its highest point. Sleepers Island was identified in Lot No. 1 of the Masonian grant.

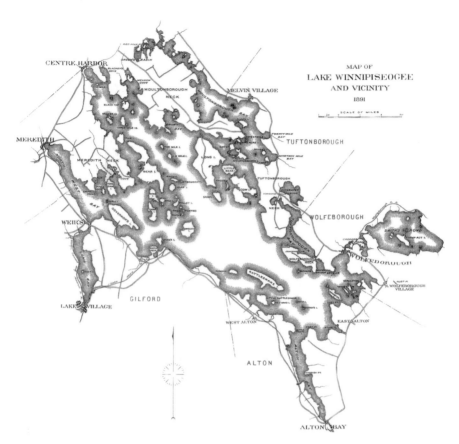

Map of Lake Winnipisieogee and vicinity, 1891. *Courtesy of the Lake Winnipesaukee Historical Society.*

COLONIAL SETTLERS

Sleepers Island was originally labeled on plans of the areas as Flanders Island after Daniel, Ezekiel and Thomas Flanders, original colonists in New Durham Gore, or "The Gore." Daniel Flanders (a cooper)—with his wife, Elizabeth Eastman Kingsbury; sons, Thomas and Ezekiel; and daughter, Sarah—purchased land in New Durham Gore in 1773, according to Flanders family history. Thomas Flanders along with Jonathan Coffin, Sarah Flanders's husband, settled on Coffin Ridge. They purchased two hundred acres, each taking one hundred acres for themselves from John Moffat in Portsmouth, New Hampshire, for £120 on November 4, 1773, according to Griffin's *The History of Alton*:

John Moffat of Portsmouth for 120 pounds lawful money, paid by Jonathan Coffin & Thomas Flanders, both of Poplin, grants a tract of land called the Gore bounded northwesterly by Gilmanton, northerly on Winnepisseokee Pond, easterly on New Durham & southwesterly on Barnstead, to contain 200 acres.

Coffin and Flanders had been neighbors in Poplin, New Hampshire (now Fremont), and ship carpenters working in Portsmouth. Coffin and Flanders additionally both worked some time at the Sheepscot River in the Wisscasset/Boothbay area of Maine, building vessels for the government. The land purchased was part of Lot No. 10 in New Durham Gore. By the end of the year, Jonathan Coffin and Thomas Flanders had built small wood-framed farmhouses within one hundred feet of each other—Jonathan on the northerly side of the road and Thomas on the opposite side of the road. Ezekiel Flanders married Mehritable Glidden in 1763 in Kingston, New Hampshire. Ezekiel and Mehritable had thirteen children, ten of whom were born in New Durham Gore (Alton). Ezekiel Flanders moved with his father and brother to New Durham Gore in 1773 and to West Alton in 1791.

The following spring, in 1774, Thomas moved north from Poplin with his father, mother, brother Ezekiel and Ezekiel's wife and family. During the summer of 1774, Jonathan, Ezekiel and Thomas built several more structures on the property and cleared land for farming and grazing. The initial house was much too small for five adults and four children, so Thomas began construction of a much larger two-story house across the newly constructed cartway that led to Gilmanton Iron Works. Ezekiel Flanders began purchasing additional land that extended to the Gilmanton town line.

The Flanders brothers are said to have had a fine farm and a fruit orchard. Thomas was described by his grandson Daniel as "a great favorite with the children of whom he was very fond. He was a man of a happy disposition and a noted entertainer with his stories of war, and witchcraft, having a fine memory." Ezekiel and Thomas fought in the Revolutionary War in the John Stark regiment. Thomas additionally fought under Washington at the Battle of White Plains, New York, and in the Battle of Trenton.

Thomas Flanders was a master shipbuilder and was hired by Charles Rodgers to build the first decked vessel of Winnipesaukee, a two-masted, white oak–frame shell. He was commissioned to build a vessel suitable for navigation on the lake, specifically for the purpose of carrying cargo and passengers from Alton Bay to Wolfeboro, where Royal Governor John Wentworth was building a summer estate. The sloop was the first on the lake and was christened the *Rockingham*. The *Rockingham* transported bricks for chimneys from Clay Point in Alton to Mast Landing in Wolfeboro during the construction of the Wentworth estate in 1769. The Wentworth estate was the oldest inland summer home in the lakes region.

The Wentworth summer home once sat on 4,300 acres owned by Governor John Wentworth and reportedly employed 150 people. The main house was 104 by 42 feet, and its beams stood more than 25 feet high. It was built with a white oak frame harvested from the local mainland and island trees. It was likely the largest house in New England at the time. Outbuildings on the property included a sawmill, two stables, a dairy, a blacksmith, joiner and cabinetmaker shops, a smokehouse, a gristmill and many more. The Wentworths were forced to flee their summer home due to threats from Loyalists who remained faithful to the king in 1774. In 1820, an old shingle that was used for kindling to start a fire landed on the roof of the home. The home was set ablaze and was never rebuilt. In 1894, the white oak frame of the *Rockingham* could still be seen on the south shore of the lake.

Thomas Flanders opposed the incorporation of New Durham Gore into Alton in 1796. Town records indicate that he felt closer to Gilmanton or New Durham than to what was developing into the Alton Village. He and fellow dissenters spoke long and earnestly for the old ways. The settlers originally proposed changing the name to Roxbury but settled on Alton, after a market town in Staffordshire, England. After seven petitions to the New Hampshire courts, the name of the town was changed from New Durham Gore to Alton, New Hampshire.

The island eventually came into the hands of Nathaniel Appleton Haven of Portsmouth, New Hampshire, and Harry L. Long of England. Nathaniel married Mary Tufton Moffat, who was a descendant of the original Masonian grantees of the state of New Hampshire, Captain Mason and John Tufton Mason. Harry L. Long was married to the granddaughter of John Thomlinson. Nathaniel Haven was a graduate of Phillips Exeter Academy and Harvard College, where he studied divinity and "classical studies." After leaving Harvard, he went to study law under Mason in Portsmouth. He was elected as a Federalist to the 11th Congress as a U.S. representative of the state of New Hampshire. Haven served from

Photo of Nathaniel Appleton Haven (1790–1826) of Portsmouth. *Courtesy of New Hampshire Historical Society.*

March 4, 1809, to March 3, 1811. Haven used his family ties to acquire several of the "original" rights from the heirs of the Masonian Proprietors who had passed away. Nathaniel Appleton Haven Jr. passed away in 1826.

By 1830, the island had become divided between two property owners, the heirs of Nathaniel Haven of Portsmouth, New Hampshire, and Harry L. Long of England. The two halves of the island were sold to David Glidden Jr. of Alton in 1833 in two separate transactions. David Glidden Jr. was a yeoman and sergeant in Captain Benjamin Whittier's militia in the defense of West Point.

In June 1833, Glidden sold one-third shares in the island to Nehemiah Sleeper Jr. and Abner Morse of Alton. The island at this time was presumably used for seasonal grazing and as a wood lot, as many of the other local islands were used for the same. In 1838, Glidden and Morse sold their shares to George W. Sanders, a Gilford lumberman and Nehemiah Jr.'s brother-in-law. Sanders also maintained ownership of the 212 unnumbered/unnamed islands, in addition to Round Island and Timber Island. Sanders owned the largest lumber yard in Gilford, and his interest in the islands was for their wood and timber supplies. Sanders retained two-thirds interest in the island until 1844, when he sold his shares to Jonas and George Sleeper of Gilford, New Hampshire, Nehemiah and Mary's sons. George Sanders continued to maintain interest and ownership in the unnumbered/unnamed islands, Round and Timber until his death while ice fishing at his Glendale camp in 1903. In 1848, Nehemiah Jr. sold his remaining interest in the island to his sons, Jonas and George, for $142. The two brothers co-owned the island jointly for twenty-one years.

Nehemiah Sleeper and Apphia Morrill had nine children: Susanna, Henry, Joseph, Lois, Jonas, Nehamiah Jr., Apphia, Hezekiah and Martha. In 1788, Nehemiah was a delegate for the Town of Hawke, New Hampshire (now Danville, New Hampshire), at the Convention of the Delegates of the People of the State of New Hampshire, where the delegates briefly discussed the writing of the U.S. Constitution. Nehemiah and Apphia relocated the Sleeper family to New Durham Gore in 1774 and settled on the lakeshore. Sleeper was a prominent town resident and was elected as town representative in 1799, 1803, 1804 and 1805. Additionally, Nehemiah was elected to be on the local school committee in two separate years, 1798 and 1809, charged with deciding on the quality of the schools and teachers in Gilmanton.

Nehemiah Jr. was born in Hawke (now Danville) and married Mary Sanders of Center Harbor, New Hampshire, in 1815. Mary's brother was local lumber magnate George W. Sanders. Nehemiah Jr. purchased a one-third share in the island in 1833 from David Glidden Jr. of Alton. Nehemiah Jr. was a farmer, and the island likely was used for seasonal grazing and as a wood lot during this time. In 1848, Nehemiah's share of the island was transferred to his two sons Jonas and George Sleeper, who had purchased the other two-thirds of the island from their uncle George Sanders. The island became locally known as "Sleepers Island"; however, the island name did not become official until 1906.

Jonas Darius Sleeper had many occupations. He was a graduate of the American and Theological Institute in New Hampton, New Hampshire, and of Brown University. He was a farmer, clerk of courts, postmaster of the West Alton Post Office (1880–81) and then collector of taxes in Alton in 1883. George Sleeper was a graduate of the New England Literary and Theological Institution in New Hampton. George owned George L. Sleeper & Company in Alton, a grocery store, and was auditor for the Town of Alton.

Jonas and George were not the only Sleepers to purchase one of the Winnipesaukee Island properties. Henry Sleeper was the grandson of Nehemiah and Apphia Morrill and cousin to Jonas and George Sleeper. Henry purchased a half share of Mark Island in 1866. Henry owned half of Mark Island until his death in 1879. Henry died bankrupt, and his share of Mark Island was sold to the Winnipesaukee Lake Cotton and Woolen Manufacturing Company (Lake Company) by a court agent.

Jonas and George Sleeper retained ownership of the island until 1869, when they conveyed the island to Sarah Worster in 1869 for the sum of ten dollars. Sarah was the wife of James Worster, who had previously purchased Rattlesnake Island in 1850. James Worster was a farmer and former blacksmith and is locally infamous for leading the fight against the Lake Company, which operated the Lakeport Dam. The dam controlled the flow of water from Winnipesaukee into the Merrimack River, which in turn powered the textile mills in Massachusetts. The Lake Company was owned by Boston Associates, the same group of people that owned the textile mills. The Merrimack River had been shaped by the company, with additional dams and canals altering its natural course for the benefit of the Massachusetts manufacturing industry. The Massachusetts textile barons additionally set up the Winnipiseogee Lake Cotton and Woolen Manufacturing Company of New Hampshire, which became known as the Lake Company.

Between 1845 and 1856, the Lake Company began purchasing land surrounding the lake and waterways leading to the Merrimack River in order to control the flow of water. The 250-foot Lakeport Dam was built in 1950 and began to control the outflow of water from Winnipesaukee into the Merrimack River. By 1857, the Lake Company had devised a system for raising and lowering the lake levels in order to send more water downriver during the dry months and keep the textile mills going. Raising the lake levels flooded farmers' fields on the lake and islands, and lowering the lake levels impeded navigation for shippers and ferryboat owners. Additionally, loggers could not send timber downstream when water levels were low. Local New Hampshire mill operations did not have enough waterpower to run their machinery.

In 1849, James Worster's daughter took the Lake Company to court for flooding her fields in Tuftonboro. This case was dismissed two years later. James Worster became obsessed with attempting to decrease Massachusetts mill owners' control over New Hampshire waterways. A Lake County agent said, "He ought to be in jail or in an insane asylum." A New Hampshire judge described him as "so much a man of one idea, that it is of no use to talk with him," according to the New England Historical Society in 2022. In 1847, Worster attacked the Salmon Falls Dam in Dover, New Hampshire, claiming damage to land he leased; Worster ripped off planking, damaged an abutment and removed stones from the dam. New Hampshire law at this time permitted landowners with properties that were flooded by mill dams to remove the nuisance structure. However, the Great Falls Company sought and won an injunction against Worster so that he could not further damage the dam.

Worster began purchasing land around Winnipesaukee, a meadowland in Sanbornton, a farm in Paugus Bay and a third of Rattlesnake Island. In 1853, Worster threatened to destroy the dam, indicating that it threatened the land he owned and leased in the surrounding villages. The courts issued an injunction in 1855 preventing Worster from tampering with the Lakeport Dam. Barred from tampering with the dams, Worster continued purchasing property around the Merrimack and Lake Winnipesaukee, purchasing in Hooksett just upstream of the Amoskeag Dam. In July 1859, James Worster, his son John Harvey and four others attempted to attack the Amoskeag Dam but were arrested on the spot, as the authorities had been tipped off to Worster's plans. Worster went on trial for attempting to destroy the Amoskeag Dam. This was the third dam and waterworks project he had made threats against or attempted to destroy in ten years.

By September 1859, the Lake Company had pulled water from New Hampshire waterways for 117 days, longer than ever before. Local farmers, including Worster, were fed up with flooded fields, lost crops and low lake levels. On September 28, 1859, Worster led fifty angry farmers, mill operators, loggers and laborers to destroy the 250-foot Lakeport Dam, which controlled the outflow of Lake Winnipesaukee. Farmers led by Worster attacked the dam with shovels and pickaxes, removing planks in the hopes of alleviating their flooded fields. The rioters were unsuccessful in destroying the dam, although they did do some damage. The Lake Company filed a suit against James Worster for the violation of the previous injunction and continued threats. In the subsequent years, Worster was tried and sentenced to three months' incarceration and a $500 fine.

Despite their defeat, the Worster family continued to purchase land around the lake. The Rattlesnake deeds were transferred to James's children, George and Susan Worster. Sleepers Island transferred ownership to James's wife, Sarah. In order to afford the purchase of Sleepers Island, Sarah received a mortgage loan from James Littlefield of Dover, New Hampshire, for the amount of $1,400. Littlefield also owned the loans of Sarah's children for the Rattlesnake Island property. Sarah fell on hard times and defaulted on the loans. Littlefield passed away in 1871, and the default went unnoticed for several years, as Littlefield's heirs did not live in New Hampshire. The Littlefield estate sued Sarah for default on the loan. The island was foreclosed on in 1877, and the property was transferred to Cyrus Littlefield et al., the heirs of James Littlefield.

The Boston and Maine Corporation began adding passenger railroad service to the lake. The Lake Shore Line connected Alton Bay to The Weirs. The final pin was nailed into the track in 1890 after thirty years of construction, opening twenty stations—Alton Bay, Keewaydin, Loon Cove, Buckley, Brookhurst, Mount Major, Woodlands, West Alton, Smith's Point, Spring Haven, Ames, Terrace Hill, Lakeshore Park, Greystone, Belknap Point, Glendale, Gilford or Sanders, Meadow Brook, Lily Pond and Lakeport—according to the *Lake Shore Bulletin* of June 17, 1890. The shores of the lake were quickly being developed as summer home properties with this increased access provided by the Lake Shore Railroad.

The heirs of James Littlefield owned Sleepers Island until 1894, when they sold the island to William Hale of Boston and Edward Pillsbury Hale of Brookfield, Massachusetts. During this four-decade period, from 1860 to 1900, the island was called both "Sleepers Island" and "Little Rattlesnake Island" depending on which map or plan was being viewed. After 1906, the island became officially known as Sleepers Island.

In the last twenty years of the nineteenth century, Sleepers Island was the location of an unusual drowning story. The steamer *James Bell* was making a night trip from Alton to Lakeport. The engineer aboard left his post to scoop up a bucket of water from the lake while passing the shore of Sleepers Island. While attempting to haul up the bucket, the engineer either lost his balance or fell overboard. The remainder of the crew were unaware of his absence until a call for reduced speed was unanswered. The only clue in the engineer's disappearance was the absence of the bucket and cord to pull water from the lake.

HALE CASTLE

In 1894, the Littlefield heirs sold the island to William and Edward Hale, the younger two of three sons of New Hampshire senator William and Mary Jane (Pillsbury) Hale of Concord, New Hampshire. Edward Buxton Hale was an 1887 graduate of Dartmouth College who became a high school principal and later a lawyer in Massachusetts. William Pillsbury Hale was an 1889 graduate of Dartmouth College, graduating with a degree in law. William practiced law in Boston, Massachusetts. In 1892, William wrote the book *Christ vs Christianity, the Christian Church Cross-Examined by a Modern Lawyer*, and lectured in the Boston area on the topic.

Photo postcard of Small's Cove Sand Bar, West Alton. *Courtesy of author.*

William would stay at the Mountain View Cottages in West Alton and make day trips to the island. The brothers shared ownership of the island until 1898, when William bought out his brother and became the sole owner of the island. On November 2, 1904, William purchased a boathouse in Rollins Cove (Glidden Cove) for $200. The purchase included a cedar rowboat and a flat-bottom skiff. The purchase also includes the right of Charles Rollins to store his boat in the boathouse free of charge until June 1, 1905, as had been previously arranged.

WILLIAM P. HALE.

Photo of William Pillsbury Hale. *Courtesy of Archive.org.*

In 1907, the Massachusetts Bar Association sought to disbar William for excessive charges to a client for her work on her divorce. William arranged a divorce settlement for $6,000 for a woman and took $3,174 in fees for his two years of work on the case. The bar association found this to be excessive and suspended him from practicing law for one year. William married Clara A. Lenker in Ohio in 1909. William was forty-two, and Clara was thirty-seven years old. They had no children. Clara was the eldest daughter of Daniel Lenker, a manufacturer, and Adaline Painter of Canton, Ohio.

The Hales began their marriage at William's home in Belmont, Massachusetts, with housekeeper and handyman couple Anna and George Pierce. William P. Hale took out two mortgages with the Merrimack River Savings Bank for the two halves of Sleepers Island in the amounts of $2,000 and $4,500. William and Clara built what became known as "Hale's Castle" in 1911 after seeing castles in Ireland on their honeymoon. The Italian stonemasons who built the Hale's Castle were the same as those who two years later built Castle in the Clouds in Moultonborough. Stones were sourced from the island itself. The castle was built on four hundred feet of frontage with five bedrooms, one and a half bathroom and four stone fireplaces. William and Clara additionally built a split-level barn that housed horses on the lower level and servants on the top level, as well as a boathouse on the shore. William maintained bridle paths around the island for his horses. In the 1960s, a horse skeleton was found on the northern side (Rattlesnake side) of the island, according to Brewer.

William and Clara lived on the island full time until her death in 1912 at the age of forty-one of "sclerosis of cord," now known as multiple sclerosis.

Clara is buried in one of the crypts at the island cemetery. After the death of his wife, William returned to an apartment in Belmont, Massachusetts, and used the island as a summer home.

In 1916, Anna Moore (Lord) Pierce, a widowed housekeeper working for William Hale, passed away on the island. Anna was the daughter of Joseph Hart Lord and Elizabeth Ruth Cheney of Cooper, Maine. Anna married George Pierce on December 15, 1878, in Quincy, Massachusetts. George worked as a butler and a property maintenance man, while Anna worked as a housekeeper in William Hale's Belmont, Massachusetts home from 1890 until her death. Anna died on May 5, 1916, at the age of fifty-seven, also from "sclerosis of spinal cord." She was interred at the island cemetery alongside Clara in Hale Cemetery. After Anna's passing, William hired Ms. Emma M. Brodeur to serve as his house staff. Emma was a former milliner in Ware and Boston. Hale Cemetery is the only known cemetery on the islands in Alton and Wolfeboro.

In August 1920, William notified his housekeeper that if he found a woman half as good as his first wife, he would marry her, and he believed that he had found such a woman. Ms. Brodeur expressed, "What is to become of me?" William reassured her that he didn't see why she couldn't remain with the couple as long as she lived, as Mrs. Pierce had. Ms. Brodeur indicated that "she could not become a common servant." William indicated that he "saw

Photo postcard of an unnamed steamer at Hale Castle on Sleepers Island, circa 1914. *Courtesy of author.*

Hale Cemetery location on the Sleeper Island Association land in the center of Sleepers Island. Hale's housekeeper Anna Moore (Lord) Peirce (1858–1916) and his first wife, Clara (Lenker) Hale (1871–1912), are buried here; the third tomb is empty. *Photo by author.*

no reason for that, that she could be a valued member of the household as my first housekeeper had been." Emma also indicated that she cared more for him than he thought, as noted in the *Boston Post* of December 18, 1920.

William set up a meeting between Ms. June C. Houston and Emma in Nantasket. Upon the boat's landing, Emma indicated that she wished to speak privately with June. The pair walked over to a pavilion to talk privately. Upon separating from William, Emma opened her handbag to show June letters that were supposedly written to Ms. Brodeur. Emma asked June if she recognized the handwriting on the letters. Emma related that the only reason William wanted to marry June was so she could help with his manuscript, as she was a high school teacher. Emma went on to say that she would ensure that the marriage never happened by destroying his manuscript. Emma proceeded to request June to use her influence over William to get him to pay her a sum of money for the letters in her possession. Emma additionally alleged to June that William was abusive toward her. Emma indicated that she had been "made black and blue on one arm and a leg where he kicked and struck her."

After the Nantasket trip, William told Emma that he would no longer be needing her services. On August 22, 1920, Emma sued William for $50,000 for breach of promise. Emma claimed that she lived with William as his fiancée, not his housekeeper, at the house in Belmont and the castle in Alton. Emma additionally claimed that the letters were not written to Clara, but rather that William had written them to her. This was not the first breach of promise suit Emma Brodeur had presented. In 1905 and 1906, she brought a $20,000 suit against widower Frank P. Clark of Ware, Massachusetts. The first suit was settled out of court; the second suit went to trial, and she was awarded $2,000 from the courts. Emma's mother also brought a $20,000 suit against Mr. Clark. Again, this suit came after Mr. Clark indicated his intent to marry another woman.

On September 2, 1920, William married June C. Houston of Marblehead, Massachusetts. June was thirty-two, and William was sixty. Upon returning to the island, William discovered that memos, letters and a portion of his manuscript was missing from the tin box where they had been stored, as well as two pongee silk dress patterns and a silk parasol. In November 1920, William sued his former housekeeper Emma Brodeur, whom he had let go back in August, over the theft of letters to his first wife, Clara; notes; clippings and memoranda; and papers relating to a historical manuscript he was writing.

Throughout the trial, Emma produced pieces of five letters but never produced the full scope of documents listed in the suit. When the letters were inspected, William indicated that the pieces of letters that were presented had been written to his mother and first wife. Emma indicated that the letters had been torn by William himself when he flew into a rage over Memorial Day that year. Several additional allegations against William were made by Emma. She indicated that she was motivated by jealousy and that William had entertained several wives of prominent New Hampshire men while on the island. She indicated that she had returned to the island to find light-colored hairpins on one of the mantelpieces in the castle, as well as feminine hair.

During the trial, June sat right next to her new husband and wrote down the pertinent information being presented, as William had previously lost his hearing. William lost the suit against Emma, but Emma's breach of promise suit was eventually dismissed. After the lawsuit, William and June set sail on the *Martha Washington* from Boston, Massachusetts, for an extended tour of Italy and southern France.

William Hale passed away in May 1936 at the age of sixty-nine after suffering a heart attack. William was buried at the Harmony Grove Cemetery in Salem, Massachusetts, and not in the island cemetery with his first wife.

The Winnipesaukee area was hit with several large weather events during the summer of 1938. On August 1, 1938, a tornado hit Gilford and Laconia. A swath of destruction a half mile wide extended from The Weirs to Bear Island. The Hotel Rose Edwards and Hotel Winnequett in The Weirs, as well as sections of the Boston and Maine Railroad tracks, sustained damage from "cyclonic" winds and downed trees. Vacationers at the Hotel Winniquett described the wind as being like "a freight train." More than one hundred pine trees fell in the weather event, and a garage was pulled from its foundation.

On September 22, 1938, what became known as the "Great New England Hurricane" hit the Winnipesaukee region. The eye of the hurricane tracked along the New Hampshire and Vermont state border at a level of Category 3. The Holiday Cabins at The Weirs were crushed by the tall pines that were spared from the previous month's tornado and splintered like "eggshells."

The federal government set up the Northeastern Timber Salvage Administration to manage the sale of the timber. The Weirs were used as they were one hundred years prior to store the logs so they wouldn't be destroyed by insects or rot. So many trees fell that the New Hampshire paper mills were still processing the trees nine years later. After the storm, the Winnipesaukee River flooded its banks, and subsequently the dams downstream on the Merrimack overflowed, flooding Concord, Manchester and Nashua, New Hampshire.

In May 1938, three years after William's death, June having lost interest in visiting the island, sold the property, including the rights to a boathouse, wharf and a right of way in Rollins Cove (now Glidden Cove) on the mainland, to Ivar Swenson. At the time of this transaction, the property was transferred for the sum of $1 and remittance of the existing mortgage of $3,500 with the Merrimack River Savings Bank.

Ivar Swenson emigrated from Malmo, Sweden, to the United States in 1904. He learned English and studied general electricity at the Pratt Institute in 1910 and electrical engineering at Columbia University. Ivar married Hilda Viola Sikora, the daughter of a house painter John Sikora and Carrie Anderson, in Arlington, Massachusetts, in 1915. After college, Ivar went to work for the General Electric Company. Ivar was given the job of estimating the cost to lay a power cable over to Sleepers Island. This first cable was run over on the ice, and the cable sank to the lakebed when the ice melted. Ivar was widowed in 1930. He married a second time to dressmaker Martha Anderson in 1937.

Ivar Swenson purchased the island in 1939 just before the hurricane hit the area. There was a tremendous amount of tree damage on the island after the hurricane, and a good deal of work was necessary to put the island back into good condition, according to the *Laconia Sun* of 2008:

> *Veazey believes the Belknap Mountain Range deflected the storm upward, sparing Laconia from the storm's worst winds. The islands on Lake Winnipesaukee weren't so fortunate, though, and many a tree was knocked over by the storm. It was the big pine trees that were most vulnerable, and when they came down, they generally took another tree or two with them. Veazey's father and grandfather, as well as the Avery family of Moultonborough, were contracted with the state's Forestry Department to log and clean up the islands. "It was a bonanza," said Veazey. The process of cleaning up the islands started in the winter, as soon as the ice was thick enough for workers to cross to the islands. The workers, called "choppers," would pull the logs out onto the ice, and when the ice melted in the summer of 1939, steamships, outfitted with booms, were employed to herd the logs to the Weirs Channel.*

The logs from the hurricane filled The Weirs. There are reports of so many logs clogging The Weirs that you were able to walk across The Weirs to the icehouse in Paugus Bay without getting your feet wet. Most of the timber ended up being processed into pulp for paper, but many of the birch logs were used during World War II to make rifle boxes, crutches and caskets; the remainder was used for firewood for locals.

Ivar would keep a glass in the boathouse at the castle and would fill it from the waters of the lake, remarking how wonderful it tasted. Ivar's granddaughter Karen vacationed on the island during the 1950s and early 1960s and had many happy childhood memories of the island and its buildings. The Swensons had a fourteen-foot Old Town runabout with all-natural wood on the forward deck and the inside. It was powered by a twenty-five-horsepower Evinrude motor. When not at the island, the boat was kept at the boathouse in Rollins Cove. The Rollins Cove boathouse has been refurbished but still sits on the same foundation adjacent to the cement pier and sandy beach.

The barn associated with the castle also contained a low-mileage 1930 Victoria coupe. The coupe was driven across the ice one winter. The rear wheel was removed to run a pulley that, in turn, ran a sawmill.

Ivar kept the island for twenty-three years until he passed away in 1962, and then the island passed to his son, John Swenson. The island and all the contents were sold the following year. There was great concern for forest

Sailing around Sleepers Island. *Courtesy of Lake Winnipesaukee Historical Society.*

fires, and fire insurance for the property was becoming too costly. The island was sold to a developer who had inquired about purchasing the island a few years before. In 1963, Ivar's son, John, sold the island and all the contents to Castlewood Corporation, which in turn divested the island into its eighty-two current parcels. It was after this that Hales Castle became known as "Castlewood." The castle and its respective outbuildings remained the only structures on the island until the mid-1960s, when the island was divested.

In the 1960s, a bed-and-breakfast called Castlewood was operated on the property. Castlewood did not rent rooms in the castle but offered rooms in the boatel and two adjacent cottages for a total of six rooms for rent. The property at this time was co-owned by the Brewer family from Wenham, Massachusetts; the Wilton Dadmum family from Danvers, Massachusetts; and Gary Paterson. Boatels—waterside hotels that were equipped with docks to accommodate people who traveled by boat—had become popular in the previous decade. Boating was seeing a boom in New Hampshire, and there were more boats than there were docks at the time. The boatels in New Hampshire were primarily related to development. Boatels were located at Treasure and Sleepers Island; Lake Sunapee had Rogers Boatel at Blodgett's Landing and Beacon Marina Boatel in Newbury, and Hampton Beach had one on Ashworth Avenue.

Guests of the boatel could rent rooms in either the boatel or two adjoining cottages to the left of the castle with dock space. The castle remained a private residence for the owners and caretakers. Guests could rent boats or be picked up by a ferry/water taxi service at the West Alton Marina for their stay at the boatel. The boatel had a snack bar and coffee shop and offered guests breakfast. The barn behind the castle had a pizza and sandwich shop. At this time, there were only three summer homes on the island, including Hale Castle. The boatel only operated for several years.

In 1963, Castlewood erected an observation tower on the summit of the island. The tower was accessed via a twenty-five-foot-wide right of way path that existed behind the castle and the properties to the northwest (Lots 80, 81 and 82). The tower boasted views of the Broads and the mainland.

In 1968, the castle itself began to be rented out. Rick Nash and his family rented it in July 1969, and he recalled watching the live feed of the Apollo 11 moon landing from a black-and-white television:

> *The summer man landed on the moon we rented the castle, and at midnight I can remember it like it was just yesterday, watching a twelve-inch black-and-white TV live coverage and they first stepped on the moon's surface for the first time. All on the point by the flagpole out front.*

The Castlewood Corporation, led by H. Ford Brewer, granted several of the properties surrounding the castle to its investors, the Dadmum family,

Hale Castle on Sleepers Island, 2019. *Photo by author.*

and the Brewers took Lot No. 4 for their own family summer home. The castle and the surrounding property were kept by Castlewood Corporation until 1971, when it was purchased by John P. and Emilie Brady. In turn, they sold it in 1977 to Robert F. and Maureen Murphy, and finally it was sold to the current owner, the Mercer family, in 1984. Over the years, the condition of the property had deteriorated, and the Mercers restored the property and continue to use the castle as their summer home.

VACATION HOME ERA

At a certain time when I'm old, I know where I'll be, wherever I am. It will be very early on a calm, warm late-June morning on Lake Winnipesaukee. I'll walk down to the water's edge below my house on Sleepers Island, rest on the bench we had built there years before, and sip from a mug of hot coffee. From the distance, I'll hear the faint sound of an outboard motor, but the huge lake before me, lying there in its myriad of undulating reflections, will be otherwise free of human activity. Then, far down near The Witches and Forty Islands, I'll see a dark, faintly ominous-looking band of ruffled water creeping slowly toward me along the entire breadth of the lake, from Meredith Bay to Moultonborough Neck. There'll be long-ago voices and laughter like distant music. A solitary leaf on the poplar tree leaning over the shore near me will flap lazily as if in preparation for the daily summertime wind–inevitably on its way, as always. While I wait for it calmly in the temporary magical stillness of early morning, just as I've done a thousand times before, I'll look across the water to the hills that rise over the faraway shores and then on and on beyond for miles and miles of misty blue mountains to the north.

—Judson D. Hale Sr., 1971

While the mainland properties show an explosion of summer camp homes around the turn of the twentieth century, most islands on the lake were not developed until the mid-twentieth century. Beginning in the mid-1950s, summer vacationing began to take off around Lake Winnipesaukee. This was fueled by national trends including population growth, economic prosperity, the evolution of the automobile and the development of reliable and affordable family boating. In 1962, the island was sold to the Sleepers Island Corporation and subdivided into eighty-two individual vacation home

Sunset off Sleepers Island, 2019. *Photo by author.*

properties. The Sleepers Island Corporation advertised the lots for thirty to fifty dollars per linear foot of shoreline.

In 1975, Sleepers Island was one of thirty stops for the *Gray Ghost* mail boat out of Wolfeboro. Mail service began on the lake in 1892 at Camp Idlewood on Cow Island. The *Gray Ghost* was operated by Alexander (Sandy) McKenzie IV and was a twenty-five-foot wooden Lyman Powercraft. The *Gray Ghost* had a fifty-four-mile route and would use the postmark "Wolfeboro-Merrymount RPO." Merrymount was a stop in Tuftonboro, and RPO stood for Railway Post Office, which was reminiscent of the days when the railways owned the lake steamers that would deliver mail on the lake. The *Gray Ghost* would leave Wolfeboro and stop at Grant Island, go around Springfield Point to the Varney Islands, Camp Kehonka, Camp Alton, Camp DeWitt in Roberts Cove and then to West Alton, Treasure Island and Sleepers Island before heading across the Broads into Winter Harbor. Deliveries would be made to residents in Winter Harbor and then around Tuftonboro Neck to Chases Island, Merrymount, Little Bear and Cow Island before returning to Wolfeboro. The *Gray Ghost* was replaced by the *Blue Ghost* in 1977.

SLEEPER ISLAND CORPORATION
Presents

SLEEPER ISLAND

ON LAKE WINNIPESAUKEE
WEST ALTON, BELKNAP COUNTY N.H.

Sleeper Island contains more than 100 acres of beautifully wooded land and there are 10,000 feet of shore line.
Water Taxi Service for Prospects

A 1965 development flyer for the real estate divestment of Sleepers Island in Alton. *Courtesy of author.*

SLEEPERS ISLAND ASSOCIATION

The Sleepers Island Association (SIA) is a voluntary, nonprofit corporation formed in 1969 by a group of shorefront property owners on Sleepers Island in Lake Winnipesaukee in West Alton, New Hampshire. It was incorporated as an association with the state in 1975, with nineteen island lot owners signing on to the association. In 1980, the final shorefront lot was sold on Sleepers Island, and Keewaydin Shores put the interior of the island up for sale. The island association voted to raise appropriate funds in order to purchase the center of the island and conserve it as forestland. Keewaydin agreed to sell the interior parcel for below market value for its conservation. In 1981, the SIA purchased the interior of the island from the Keewaydin corporation for $15,000. The land was designated as conservation land. The association's purpose is to preserve the center of the island, about sixty acres, in its natural state (except for septic easements in the perimeter), to provide fire protection on the island as a supplement to the town's service and to provide social activities for its members. Island association members voted to raise dues, and each paid $150 per year for three years to fund the purchase and mortgage on the property.

The association purchased the first of four fire pumps for the island in 1980. Fire service response at this time was fifty-five minutes. Island resident Jud Hale built the first pump house for the pump, which was located at the rear of his property, and painted it red. Working with the Alton fire chief Kopp, the association built and outfitted a total of four Indian fire pumps, two hundred feet of fire hoses and associated firefighting gear in four fire pump houses located around the island. As island residences changed hands over the years and fire response time to the island was reduced to eighteen minutes, it became clearer that the association did not need to continue maintaining the fire pumps and pump houses. The association found that the pumps were heavy, unreliable and not being maintained on a regular basis, and their use was officially discontinued in 2016. The fire pump houses began to be dismantled in 2022.

In 1993, a recreation walking trail of about two miles around the center of the island was created by members of the association. Additional trails were added to the island trail network in 2020 and 2022.

RATTLESNAKE ISLAND

Rattlesnake Island comprises 290 acres and is the fifth-largest island in Lake Winnipesaukee. It is located about two miles from shores of West Alton and Smalls Cove and two miles from the shores of Wolfeboro Neck at the edge of the Broads. The island stretches almost two miles from east to west and is about a quarter mile wide from north to south. Rattlesnake Island has the highest elevation of all the islands on Lake Winnipesauke, reaching 791 feet above msl, or 370 feet above the average lake level.

COLONIAL SETTLERS

Rattlesnake Island shares much of its original ownership with Sleepers Island. Unlike many of the other islands in the southern Lake Winnipesaukee, there are no other known English names for Rattlesnake Island. The name comes from the Abenaki name *sisikwai (sisiquoi) menahan*, which directly translates to Rattlesnake Island. Rattlesnake Island was first identified in the 1788 Blanchard Map of the Lake Winnipesaukee watershed. It was the only island identified by name on the plan. Two theories have been presented on the naming of Rattlesnake. The first is that the topography of Rattlesnake looks like the rattles on a rattlesnake, and the second is the prevalence of timber rattlesnakes found on the island prior to 1940.

In 1781, Rattlesnake Island was divided into two parcels. The eastern portion (Lot No. 1) was deeded to Tomlinson and Marsh, and the western portion (Lot No. 2) was deeded to Mark Hunting Wentworth. Mark Hunting Wentworth was the father of Governor John Wentworth. He was a merchant and produced large quantities of masts and spars for the British navy. Rattlesnake Island was particularly important for his business as it had a plethora of old-growth timber to be used for masts. His various businesses had allotted him a large fortune, and he purchased a two-fifteenths share of the Mason Patent.

The western end of the island transferred through the Wentworth heirs to Major Francis Gore and his wife, Annabelle Wentworth. Major Francis Gore was a major in the 17th Light Dragoons, was later elected as governor of Bermuda and in 1806 was appointed as the governor of Upper Canada. In 1799, the Gores sold their half of the island to Eleazer Davis of Alton, who had also purchased Governors Island and a large parcel of mainland. Davis would use the islands for seasonal grazing of his livestock and as a source of timber. Upon Davis's death in 1826, the land passed down to his son John Davis of Alton.

Lot No. 1—which included the eastern portion of Rattlesnake and the islands of Big and Little Barndoor, Sleepers and Diamond Islands—passed into the hands of Harry Long and Nathaniel Haven of Portsmouth. Long and Haven divested the islands as individual transactions, and the eastern half of Rattlesnake was transferred through local Alton and Wolfeboro families until 1830, when both halves come under the ownership of John Davis of Alton. Davis sold the entire island in August 1830 to Nathaniel Rogers, descendant of one of the original sixty proprietors of Kingswood, William Rogers. One winter, William Rogers spent most of his time fishing on the lake. He constructed a three-sided lean-to to protect him from the wind and cold on the ice. While William could not hold laborious jobs due to injuries sustained as a soldier and hunter, he did considerable business buying and selling land around the lake.

Nathaniel Rogers allowed fellow Wolfeboro resident and founding member of the church Jesse Whitton to hunt rattlesnakes on the island. Whitton is described as an enthusiastic and demonstrative religionist. Whitton claimed knowledge in the healing arts, and his plastics and decoctions of roots and herbs were often more effective than the modern medicines of the time. While of small stature, he was incredibly agile and told stories of his prowess as a snake wrestler even into his advanced years. He has been described as an "eccentric individual, pursuing the avocation of a snake hunter." Whitton captured large numbers of rattlesnakes and extracted their venom. Rattlesnake venom was touted as a "remedial agent" for rheumatism. Whitton held the title of doctor despite having the lack of education and diploma. His practice was limited to healing ailments using herbs and rattlesnake venom.

When Nathaniel Rogers was twenty-five, his father passed away, leaving his estate to Nathaniel, his eldest son. Nathaniel took over the estate and the rearing of his younger siblings and was described as "capable and busy man," constantly improving his farm to increase its value. His first task was to build a house, which he completed in 1812. Rogers was also in charge of the sawmill at the lower falls of the Smith River and ran his mill with a double crew to produce enough lumber. Much of the timber for his sawmill came from Rattlesnake Island. Judge Rogers later went on to open one of the first stores in Wolfeboro. Nathaniel married twice, first to Mary Martha Durgin Rust and second to Eleanor Jane Piper. He had ten children between the two marriages.

In 1840, Rogers sold two-thirds of the island to Alpheus Swett of Tuftonboro. Swett was married to Nathaniel's younger sister Susan. Swett was a lumberman and farmer and owned the steam Mill Company with Moses and Augustus Varney and Benjamin Morrison. Swett used the island as a source of timber for the sawmills, increasing demands for lumber to build new homesteads and summer homes. Swett also was at one time the owner of the *James Bell*, a sidewheel steamship that had the capacity to hold 350 passengers. The *James Bell* was powered by a one-cylinder steam engine that drove the paddlewheels through a linkage of maple gears. *James Bell* was the first of the lake steamers to have interior window blinds. Swett sold the *James Bell* to investors in Lake Village who docked it at Lakeport. The *James Bell* ran aground in 1885 in the channel between the Mainland and Sleepers Island while carrying a load of wood pilings. The steamer was refloated after some time, transported to The Weirs and hauled out of the lake. The following year, the *James Bell* sank in the wharf at Lake Village. It went on to have a second life on shore as a makeshift residence for summer visitors.

Nathaniel Rogers developed the western end of the island as a farm. Pigs, sheep and cattle were raised on the island. Livestock were driven across the ice to the island. Agricultural crops like potatoes were planted on the land. Hay was grown on the island, and both the potatoes and hay were transported to the mainland by horseboat built by Rogers. The first horseboat on the lake was developed by David Parsons of Long Island. A horseboat was also used as the judge's boat for the first Harvard-Yale boat race in Center Harbor in 1856. The horseboat contained two paddlewheels built from timber on the island and a treadmill that two horses walked on to propel the paddlewheels.

The hay was stored in the barn that was previously located at the site of the Catholic church. Rattlesnakes from the island would hide in the hay bales and travel to the mainland. Rogers used pigs to control the rattlesnakes on the island. At one point, after the potatoes were loaded, the wind picked up and the waves increased, and the horseboat was overcome and sunk. Judge Rogers rode a log to the mainland and brought back help to raise the boat.

The farmhouse was a story and a half and located on the western end of the island, toward the Broads. The farmhouse was later moved across the ice to 19 Mill Street in Wolfeboro. On the island, the original cellar holes of the farmhouse could be traced to the 1950s.

At his death in 1848, Judge Rogers's estate was transferred to his daughter Martha and her husband, Silas Durgin. There was only one residence on the island at the time, a farm occupied by the grandfather of Henry Forrest Libby. In 1858, Solomon Cole of Lake Village exhibited two rattlesnakes that had been killed on Rattlesnake Island. One of these snakes was reported to have fifteen rattles, was four feet, eight inches long and was seven and a quarter inches in circumference. Over the years, more reports were seen of seven-foot-long rattlesnakes with thirteen rattles.

On July 12, 1886, local newspapers reported that a large swath of second-growth timber on Rattlesnake Island was on fire; no structures were reported on the island at the time of the fire. Fish and camp houses were located on the shoreline. The wildfire burned for three days before being extinguished by a summer rainstorm. Reports estimate that two-thirds of the timber on the island was burned. Estimates of the timber losses were between $12,000 and $15,000, and locals reported rattlesnakes swimming to other islands and the mainland to escape the fire. One newspaper reported that the island had previously burned forty years prior.

Whitten and Cole were not the only Wolfeboro residents to capitalize on the rattlesnakes on the island. John Rogers, son of Nathaniel Rogers, captured a live rattlesnake on the island in August 1894. He named the rattlesnake "Sweet Marie." Sweet Marie was exhibited around town. In the autumn, the snake was placed in a cool cellar where it hibernated for the winter. Status reports on Sweet Marie's health and wellness were reported in the local paper the following year, as on December 25, 1895: "'Sweet

Marie' the captive rattlesnake is taking his cold weather snooze. The boys have warmed him up once just to see where he was at. He was there and make no mistake about it."

In July 1900, the island was sold to Dr. Henry Forrest Libby, a dentist practicing in Boston. Dr. Libby was the son of Moses Libby of Wolfeboro and an ancestor of Reuben Libby, another of the original settlers of Wolfeboro. Reuben Libby came to Wolfeboro from New Durham and settled on one hundred acres of John Parkers land. He choose the lot on the neck that extended farthest into the lake to be near the water route between Alton and Moultonborough. Reuben was active in town matters and within a year was managing affairs on John Parkers farm. Libby was a member of the board of selectmen and sent to represent Moultonborough, Tuftonboro, Wolfeboro and Ossipee with the legislature. Reports indicate that he was an avid bear hunter, killing thirty-six in one season. Dr. Libby held the title of "doctor" despite never completing his schooling. In 1890, Dr. Libby began to focus on a study of flora and fauna, and he began to collect local specimens, studying the anatomy of both animals and humans. Dr. Libby's collection quickly began to overflow this family cottage and boathouse.

Dr. Libby and his brother John H. operated the passenger steamers *West Wind* and the *Mohawk*. They were two sister pleasure steamers that were built by George Whitney in 1889. The steamers had a steam-operated musical whistle. The Libby brothers operated them for "pleasure parties" and their own private use to travel to and from Rattlesnake and the other islands and ports of the lake. A July 8, 1889 advertisement in the *Granite State News* stated, "Wanted at once. A lady cook on the steamer Mohawk. Must be good-looking, agreeable and willing to assist the captain. Apply to Capt. John Libby."

The steamers had the capacity for up to fifty passengers, fourteen of whom could dine at a table in the cabin. The *Granite State News* reported on May 4, 1901, that Dr. Libby chartered the *West Wind* for a fishing excursion with his brother as captain. The fishing expedition netted 20 trout and 2 salmon. The *West Wind* made the news again in 1902, when passengers aboard caught 128 trout in three weeks. The *Mohawk* was later sold to Dr. D.F. Greene of Windemere on Long Island in Moultonboro. The *West Wind* was sold in 1906 and in later years was operated by John Goodhue and then subsequently Edward Lavallee, who also owned the *Mount Washington*.

Libby wanted to establish an arboretum to protect the trees on Rattlesnake Island native to the lake's region. During this time, to ready the island as a natural arboretum, he moved the one-and-a-half-story

Pre-1908 photo postcard of Diamond Island and Rattlesnake Island. *Courtesy of author's collection.*

farmhouse from the island to his street of buildings on the mainland. Once on the mainland, the house was given the address of 19 Libby Street, and a full second floor was added. The home still exists today, and town records indicate that it doesn't sit correctly on its foundation, likely due to its move across the ice from its original build location. Mr. Morrison of Wolfeboro brought forth an act to protect the "Libby Reservation" on Rattlesnake to the New Hampshire House of Representatives in 1905. However, the House determined that it was "inexpedient" or not practical to move forward with the legislation.

Libby shifted his priorities to opening a summer museum to display his collections. In order to finance the construction, he logged the timber on Rattlesnake. Dr. Libby entered a deal with Henry D. Yeaton & Company of Boston and Clifton Loring to sell all the trees, wood and logs on the island in 1910. Libby gave them six years to complete the work. Libby's hope was to prevent the destructive fires and help in the process of natural reseeding of the island. A shoreline swath of trees forty feet from the high-water mark were kept as a windbreak, and a one-acre stand of "Appalachian hemlocks" was reseeded on the western ridge of the island. Some of the hemlocks in the one-acre stand measured nine feet in circumference.

The timber company unfortunately brought along hitchhikers on its barges and boats: rats. The rats were a natural predator to the rattlesnakes, and any remaining rattlesnakes on the island were killed by the new invasive species. The money generated from the sale of timber on the island went toward Libby's new project, the Libby Museum.

Dr. Libby, after retiring in 1912, built, maintained and opened the Libby Museum in Wolfeboro. At the time, the Libby Museum contained the largest and most complete collection of New Hampshire flora and fauna. Dr. Libby devoted his retirement to the study and preservation of natural history and used his knowledge of creating plaster molds to mount exhibits in the museum. The Libby Museum had several taxidermized rattlesnakes in a diorama that described their natural habitat that were on display in the museum collections. By 1932, no rattlesnakes could be found on the island.

The small island is Diamond and the long one is Rattle Snak and the Point that runs into the lake is [handwritten caption on postcard]

Photo postcard of Diamond Island and Rattlesnake Island, circa 1910. *Courtesy of author's collection.*

Mary Ellen MacDonald of Boston filed a suit against New Hampshire state senator and local wholesale lumberman Ellsworth Hyde Rollins in 1922 over the previous logging of Rattlesnake Island. Rollins owned the Hebert Emerson farm in Loon Cove and was co-owner of Lovett & Rollins.

MacDonald was awarded $11,365.53 in the suit. The judge found that Mrs. MacDonald was entitled to a stumpage of $4 per one thousand feet for 2,536,832 board feet of timber and interest for six years, seven months on the sum. Of the total awarded, Rollins had only paid MacDonald $2,000.

Concord Silver manufacturer and pilot Spencer Treharne took over the Libby estate on Rattlesnake Island in 1936. Treharne immediately engaged fellow pilot Charles B. Baughan to fly New Yorkers to the island for winter sports.

In 1946, the Libby family granted the Boy Scout troop in Wolfeboro to use the island as a semi-permanent camping area. The Boy Scout troop under the supervision to Winston Hamm developed several campsites, and the trails were widened and opened up. The original trails on the island were created by Girl Scout campers on Camp Treasure Island. As the Boy Scouts were developing camping sites, they unearthed the old logging roads, but the roads were not cleared in order to maintain the natural beauty of the island.

The island passed through the Libby family and their heirs until April 28, 1950.

VACATION HOME ERA

Joseph Melanson of Wolfeboro purchased the island in 1950. Melanson was the son of Joseph I. Melanson, a shoe manufacturer with the Joseph I. Melanson and Brothers Company in Lynn, Massachusetts. Melanson was an amateur golf champion and the former state bridge champion. Melanson became a prominent developer of shorefront properties in the lake region. Melanson later became the president of the Wolfeboro National Bank.

Melanson was the first to attempt to develop the island into summer camp properties. Lots were initially opened as seasonal rents for tents. Yearly leases ranged from $50 to $120. Melanson later allowed renters to erect tent stands and then later build tent platforms and small cabins, and he would give rental discounts to induce renters to purchase lots and contribute toward brushing out and cleaning up the lots. All structures needed to be removed at the end of the lease or they would become the property of Melanson. Some of the original structures on the island are the remnants of the old cabins and tent platforms built by the lot renters. Melanson had plans to bring electricity to each lot and provide community docks, beaches and breakwaters. Melanson included ferry service and telephone service to the rental camps.

A 1955 flyer for leasing camping lots on Rattlesnake Island prior to the divestment of the island into individual private summer home lots. *Courtesy of Winnipesaukee Forum.*

Names of community docking areas on the island included "Major View," "Buckskin Cove," "POWWOW," "Wigwam," "Raccoon Point," "Youngs Cove," "Copelands Cove," "Washington View," "Broadview," "Longview," Mountain View" and "Birch Grove."

In June 1960, Lincoln Adams Sr. and his family were on their annual camping trip to Rattlesnake Island when his wife was injured with deep lacerations on a sharp rock on the campsite about twelve feet from the water's edge. Determined to eliminate future hazards from the area, Lincoln and his son Link Jr. decided to dig a hole and roll the sharp rock in to bury the sharp edges.

While excavating their hole, they encountered a layer of soot and ash just below the ground surface. The family, having been interested in archaeology, took great care in excavating the hole, curious to figure out the mystery of the soot and charcoal. At a depth of sixteen inches, Adams encountered fragments of burnt pottery. The fragments formed a bowl with a serrated edge and linear incised lines. Fragments included finger bones, a semi-grooved small axe and a stone arrowhead flint (celt). Lincoln, a collector of indigenous artifacts, determined that this was an indigenous cremation site that dated between the Late Woodland period (BC 500–CE 1650) and the Early Historic Occupation (CE 1541–present).

At twenty inches in depth, the Adamses reached the base of the pit, which was lined with flat, round slabs of granite that were fitted together in a circle that measured four feet, six inches in diameter. Lincoln and Link determined that the site contained no more to learn, rolled the offending rock into their excavation and backfilled with the excavated debris. The Adams family dug several additional test pits around their campsite in the following years but never found another archaeological site. Neighboring campsites found fragments of stone flints (celts). Lincoln shared his collected artifacts at local libraries in the following decades, and many of his relics are now located in collections at the New Hampshire Historical Society and New Hampshire Archaeological Society.

The Rattlesnake Island Development Corporation was formed in 1961 to develop the island into individual vacation home properties. However, it took another ten years until a subdivision plan was created for the island. The development corporation purchased the Ewing property on the mainland to provide mainland access and docking for island residents, as well as a lot on neighboring Sleepers Island to provide electric service to Rattlesnake.

The Rattlesnake Island Association was formed to protect the internal land of the island, its land on Sleepers and the mainland launch access for residents. In 2023, the Rattlesnake Island Association listed its Sleepers Island parcel for sale, no longer needing the property to supply electrical service. Electrical service to the island had been upgraded and rerouted, and the lot was no longer a needed asset. One of the internal lots on Rattlesnake was purchased by the Lakes Region Conservation Trust (LRCT).

DIAMOND ISLAND

Diamond Island is a conical island rising 584 feet above msl, or 80 feet above mean lake level. Diamond Island was part of the Masonian Proprietors Lot No. 1, with the Barndoor Islands, Sleepers Island and the eastern end of Rattlesnake Island. Diamond Island is unnamed on Hersey's 1772 map. The first instance of the name is seen by 1820s, likely named due to its conical shape.

Diamond Island, with the other Lot No. 1 islands, transferred ownership several times until it came into the ownership of James Ames, who purchased the island from Haven and Peirce. James Ames owned a large farm (Ames Farm) on the Gilford mainland that was on the opposite shore of the island. The island provided Ames with additional grazing and a source of wood.

In 1830, James Ames sold the island to his neighbor Benjamin Thurston, who continued to use the island for seasonal grazing and wood. Thurston owned the island for five years before selling it to Nathaniel Folsom (of the Wolfeboro Folsom family), who owned the island for the next thirty years. Blake Folsom owned Little Barndoor Island in the late nineteenth century.

During this time, Diamond was used for seasonal grazing and a source of timber. The Winnipesaukee Steamboat Company purchased Diamond Island from Folsom in 1865 after leasing it for four years. The steamboat company was looking to expand its business on the *Lady of the Lake* by providing a unique destination stop on the lake for tourists. The company planned to build the Diamond Island Hotel. The Diamond Island Hotel was set to be open year-round and extend excursions that the company offered.

Photo of Diamond Island. *Courtesy of author.*

DIAMOND ISLAND HOTEL

In the mid-1800s, Winnipesaukee was quickly becoming one of the first resort areas. The Boston and Maine Railroad Company operated the *Lady of the Lake* for excursions on the lake. Bear and Diamond Island were the first two island destinations as stops for the *Lady of the Lake* steamship.

Trains from Concord would stop at The Weirs in Laconia, and passengers would board the steamship for excursions on the lake for a fare of one dollar. A home, the Diamond Island House, was erected in 1861 on the island for summer shore excursionists. Passengers could spend two or five hours on shore or stay overnight in the accommodations. The Diamond Island House boasted a bowling alley and dancing pavilion among its amenities. The house had its own icehouse and was a popular Civil War–era hostelry. The Diamond Island House was open year-round for tourists.

The islands and their shores became known for their berries. "Few places in the country can equal these islands for the quantity and quality of these berries," noted the B&M Railroad Company in 1886. Low bush blueberries in July and the August huckleberries or whortleberries drew excursions for locals and tourists to the island shores for fishing, berry picking and picnic dinners. The *Lady of the Lake* route between Diamond Island and The Weirs became a popular route for excursionists. Passengers would crowd the upper decks, and the "steamer would tip until the women folk and nervous people were almost panic stricken," according to the

Laconia Democrat in 1894. It was reported that one trip carried 1,280 people from Diamond Island to The Weirs.

The Winnipesaukee Steamboat Company hired Warren W. Rider, a former confectioner from Concord, to manage the Diamond Island Hotel. Rider and his wife, Mary, lived on the island year-round, and the hotel became extremely popular with winter fishermen, who were looking for more comfortable fishing lodging as opposed to "roughing it." The hotel had two clerks, Michael Hunt of Ireland and Thomas Doe of Nottingham, New Hampshire. Thomas's wife Mary (Wallis) of Haverhill, New Hampshire, served as the hotel's cook.

Rider died of typhoid fever in 1870 while on the island; he was forty-one years old. The *Lake Village Times* reported that "the announcement of his death will cause a throb of genuine sorrow in many a heart and many a traveler over our beautiful Lake." The management of the hotel changed several times after Rider's death. However, by the 1870s, the hotel had become known for gambling and rum. In 1880, the Winnipesaukee Steamboat Company sold the island to Winborn A. Sanborn, a former company shareholder and captain of the *Lady of the Lake*.

In order to attract a higher clientele and year-round visitors, Sanborn chose to move the Diamond Island House across the lake to be part of the Hotel Weirs in 1880. In February 1880, the Diamond Island House was

DIAMOND ISLAND HOUSE IN 1861

Photo postcard of the Diamond Island House, circa 1861, showing the *Lady of the Lake* on the island docks. *Courtesy of the author.*

cut in half and moved across the ice. Just as it reached the shore in The Weirs, it broke through the ice and had to be pulled out with local oxen. It was rebuilt as Sanborn's House in The Weirs by Captain W.A. Sanborn and catered to the elite. Under the ownership of Dr. J. Alonzo Greene, the hotel was expanded to become the 350-room Hotel Weirs. The hotel burned in November 1924 when a fire that began in the music hall spread and destroyed twelve structures in The Weirs, including the new Hotel Weirs.

After the hotel was moved, there are only reports of picnickers visiting the old wharf on the island and no permanent island residents. The island remained in the ownership of Sanborn's daughter Ellen Wadleigh until her death in 1898. Fred W. Hoyt of Fernandina Beach, Florida, acquired the island from Ellen's estate.

THE SPOONER FAMILY

In 1934, Frederick Carroll Spooner, a hosiery business owner from Lincoln, Massachusetts, purchased Diamond Island for $5,000 from the estate of Fred Hoyt. Before he could finalize his purchase, he needed to prove that he could afford payments of $50 per month for two years. The Spooner family had been vacationing on Lake Winnipesaukee for several years prior. The Spooner family pitched an old army tent on the hill and would row over supplies from Batchelder's Cottage in West Alton.

The first year the Spooner family was on the island, they built a tent platform, an outdoor fireplace and a shed to house an icebox. Carroll's son David was in charge of hauling the water from the lake to the campsite in buckets. Carroll would shut down his hosiery business for a month and go work on his island property. Soon, he had constructed a log home from the Norway pine that grew on the island. It took two years for the footprint of the cabin to be completed, and in the third year, the first floor was laid. Every log was notched by hand, and it took almost one day to lay one log.

The Spooner family was active in scouting and would invite the local camps to visit the island. Boy Scouts from Camp Manning in Gilmanton would spend every Tuesday night on the island. They would leave Alton Bay and paddle up to the island and back. Girl Scouts from Treasure Island would also paddle to the island and camp overnight.

In 1938, the Great New England Hurricane hit Diamond Island. A large swath of trees across the island was destroyed. Carroll Spooner reportedly

Sarah Welcome (Baker) Spooner (1889–1983), David Baker Spooner (1928–2022) and Frederick Carroll Spooner (1894–1983) on the shores of Diamond Island during the construction of their cottage, circa 1939. *Courtesy of the Lake Winnipesaukee Historical Society.*

Sarah Welcome (Baker) Spooner, David Baker Spooner and Frederick Carroll Spooner taking a ride around Diamond Island. *Courtesy of Lake Winnipesaukee Historical Society.*

took down a half million board feet of lumber after the storm. To help with the hurricane cleanup, Raymond Dube transported two of his horses to the island, Ned and Jerry. At one point, six teams of horses were working to clear the island from the storm's destruction. Unfortunately, a visiting tourist fed a bad apple to Jerry and caused a severe case of colic. Jerry passed away and was buried on the island near the location of the old hotel.

The lumber was dragged to the shore of the island and piled up. The plan was to dynamite the log pile and send it into the water to be towed by the Swallow and Captain John Goodhue, but the dynamite did not budge the log pile. Instead, the logs had to be rolled by hand one at a time into the lake to be towed away to the mainland. The family worked all summer to remove the logs from the island and haul them to Meredith, where the Diamond Match Company purchased them to use to make matches.

Work on the cabin commenced again, and the cabin was finally complete in 1946, eleven years after it began. The cabin featured a central fireplace and a large front porch.

VISIBILITY LABORATORY

In 1947, a research group organized and directed by optical physicist Dr. Siebert Quimby Duntley of the Massachusetts Institute of Technology (MIT) was contracted by the U.S. Navy to conduct research on the penetration of daylight into oceans and lakes and on the visual sighting of underwater objects by swimmers and aviators. The research continued his wartime projects concerning the visual search for shallowly submerged objects, such as hazards to navigation as seen from low-flying aircraft and downed pilots.

After a search of locations in New England to conduct his research, he focused on Diamond Island, owned by MIT alum Frederick Spooner. The Diamond Island Field Station for the Visibility Laboratory was constructed on the southern section of the island and included two observation towers, an underwater track, a boathouse, a stone wharf, a breakwater and several small buildings used for photography, a shop and electronics. Frederick Spooner helped to build several of the field station buildings with the group from MIT and the U.S. Navy. Subsequent experiments were also conducted in Key West, Florida, by the team.

Diamond Island and the waters of Lake Winnipesaukee provided ideal conditions for the experiments to be conducted at minimal cost. A

Massachusetts Institute of Technology (MIT) and U.S. Navy personnel of the Visibility Laboratory on the docks at the Diamond Island Field Station, circa 1949–58. *Courtesy of the Lake Winnipesaukee Historical Society.*

photometer was anchored in an underwater window on a floating barge. An underwater lamp with a one-thousand-watt incandescent "diving lamp" was installed underwater. A train of nine black-painted wooden rafts, each ten feet long, was attached to the barge in front of the photometer window. These nine rafts supported the light sources. Experiments were conducted on evenings when moonlight was not present in order to ensure that no ambient light entered the photometer.

The first decade (1948–58) of the laboratory's existence focused on "daylight," the light that is generated by the sun that penetrates the water in the photic zone. The effects on the light scattering under water, the photographic clarity and the effect of wave action on the light were several of the concepts studied at the Diamond Island lab. Experiments were initially conducted with submerged incandescent bulbs. Experiments found that visibility of submerged objects was directly affected by waves. Duntley's team began a series of experiments on the electrical measurements of wave slope heights while on Diamond Island. This growing interest in optical oceanography led to the movement of the main lab to California.

The field station on Diamond Island was overseen by MIT until 1952, when Duntley was invited by Scripps Institute of Oceanography to move the laboratory from MIT to California. Using funds from the U.S. Navy, the laboratory was moved across the country to the unoccupied navy barracks

Staff of the Visibility Laboratory at the Diamond Island Field Station, circa 1949–58. *Courtesy of Lake Winnipesaukee Historical Society.*

in Point Loma. The field station then came under the jurisdiction of the University of California and Scripps.

The second decade of research (1959–66) was the most extensive and focused on underwater light and the illumination of structures and objects. Experiments with underwater lasers began in 1964 and continued until the laboratory closed. Three Radio Corporation of America (RCA) lasers were installed in the waters off Diamond Island for naval research. An underwater rail track was installed, and researchers would roll replica model submarines on the track from shallow water to deeper water and ping them with lasers. Much of the work was conducted by scuba divers who would travel from the mainland each day for work on the island.

Frank B. Isaacson, head of the Physics Branch for the Office of Naval Research (ONR), made many field visits to the Diamond Island Field Station, as did other ONR physicists such as Francis T. Byrne, Thomas B. Dowd, Charles E. Steerman and Bruce A. Finlaysen.

The underwater lasers at Diamond Island were additionally used with permission by other scientists for their independent research. Much of the technology that NASA, airports and meteorologists use to determine the visibility of an area was originally researched at the Diamond Island Field Station.

As the research began increasing in scope and depth, the results of the research began to show that light would scatter less in ocean water than in freshwater and that the Diamond Island Field Station would not be able to produce the required engineering data to produce and construct underwater lasers. The laboratory closed on the island after the summer of 1966, and the research was moved to the Scripps Laboratories in San Diego, where it could be conducted on a smaller scale when an applicable saltwater location could not be identified to meet the group's experimental needs.

The U.S. Navy took over operation of the Diamond Island Field Station and in 1969 began experiments in underwater optics and acoustics. Taxes began to increase, and the Spooner family began leasing out seasonal lots on Diamond Island. Carroll had a surveyor come out and survey the island in 1970 and offered the lessees the option to purchase their lot. Everyone who was leasing took the option to purchase their land. Diamond Island is currently divided into twenty-six individual summer home properties.

TREASURE ISLAND
AND CUB ISLAND

Treasure and Cub Islands were included in the Masonian grant as one of the unnumbered islands. Treasure Island has been known as Redhead Island and Birch Island prior to being officially named Treasure Island in 1938 by the State of New Hampshire. Treasure Island contains eleven acres of relatively flat land with a maximum elevation of 518 feet above msl, or 12 feet above average lake level. Cub Island was deeded with Treasure Island until the islands were divested into twenty-five individual summer home properties.

COLONIAL HISTORY

The first record of ownership on the islands was that of George Sanders, a Gilford lumber man. George also owned a partial interest in Sleepers Island and Rattlesnake Island at the time. Sanders likely used the island as a source of white pine and oak timber, which were in high demand for summer home construction around the lake. The island was sold to David Glidden and then to Jonas and George Sleeper. In 1869, the Treasure, Rattlesnake and Sleepers Islands came into the hands of Sarah Worster, who took out of mortgage with the Littlefield family of Portsmouth. Worster defaulted on the mortgage, and the islands came under ownership

Sailing around Sleepers Island and Cub Island in West Alton. *Courtesy of Lake Winnipesaukee Historical Society.*

by the Littlefield family. The island was subsequently purchased in 1878 by Charles Foss of Alton and then purchased in 1893 by Joseph Edward Burtt of Malden, Massachusetts. Burtt owned the ship brokerage form of Burtt and Johnson.

A new cottage was built on the island shortly after the Burtt family took ownership. During their ownership, a boathouse, icehouse and other outbuildings were constructed on the island. The Burtt family owned the island until 1913, when it was sold to L. Theodore Wallis of Brookline, Massachusetts.

Camp Mishe Mokwa

In 1914, L. Theodore Wallis opened Camp Mishe Mokwa (named for "great white bear" in the Longfellow poem *Song of Hiawatha*) on Red Head Island. Wallis was a Dartmouth College graduate and schoolteacher at the Browne and Nichols School in Cambridge, Massachusetts. Wallis strove to give the young men an "all around muscular development" while at camp. Mishe Mokwa offered nine weeks of "healthy, happy, profitable outdoor life."

Treasure Island
A Poem of Mishe Mokwa by Arthur Hammond

We used to read, when youngsters, stirring tales of pirates bold,
With their bags of buried treasure and the hoards of hidden gold.
And, in imagination, we would sail the southern sea
And dream of deeds of valor and think what fun 'twould be
To join the bold, bad buccaneers; be captain of the band,
And find a little island with a coral reef and sand,
With a cunning little harbor, where our ship could not be found,
And there we'd hide the treasure, in a cave 'way underground.
And there we'd fight the natives, and kill them by the score,
And then set sail and roam the sea until we found some more.
We loved such tales as these, and, even now, when we are old,
The thought of such an island makes us wish those pirates bold
Had left some hidden treasure caves a little nearer home,
So we could go and find them, and not have so far to roam.
Now, if you'll listen carefully, I'll tell what I know
About a treasure island you can find it you will go
To a lake among the mountains that the Indians knew so well,
Where, even to the present day, the Indian spirits dwell.
There's a little wonder island in a corner of the lake;
It is close to Sleeper's Island and not far from Rattlesnake.
You can see it from Mount Major, when it's clear and sunny weather,
And it's there the Mishe Mokwa campers love to get together.
There are hoards of golden sunshine and a treasure store of health,
And you get it all for nothing, though it's worth all kinds of wealth.
And there we live the simple life that only campers know,
With those happy, carefree youngsters with their faces all aglow.
The time goes by too rapidly, so filled up are the days

Young Mishe Mokwa camper with a toy boat on the shores of Treasure Island. *Courtesy of Lake Winnipesaukee Historical Society.*

With work and play that helps us all in many, many ways.
The work is so enjoyable that when the summer's done
We really find, instead of work, we've had a lot of fun.
We do not wear our Sunday clothes, nor have our trousers pressed,
We only need a coat of tan to be correctly dressed.
Oh! it's pippin' in the summer-time to be on Treasure Isle.
It's got all other kinds of pleasure beaten by a mile.
If you ask me what I'm going to do when summer comes again,
I'm going to pack my duffel bag and take an early train
And get to Treasure Island just as quickly as can be,
For there isn't any island in the world I'd rather see.

Wallis was in the business of "physical development of boys" and was the director of the Brown and Nichols School in Cambridge, Massachusetts. Camp activities included tennis, baseball, photography, exploring, gymnastic stunts, fishing, building boats and shacks, mountain climbing, archery, shooting range, swimming and other camp sports. A 1937 brochure even advertised horseback riding. Most of the activities at the camp happened along the shore. The camp operated a thirty-six-foot speed boat, *Grey Wolf*, with a seventy-horsepower engine. Camp Mishe Mokwa had several smaller motorboats for shorter trips and a fleet of Old Town canoes. In later years, the camp purchased a fleet of eighteen-foot Cape Cod Baby Knockabout sailboats. Once boys had mastered swimming, they needed to test their prowess by swimming to Cub Island. Once a camper had learned and mastered swimming, they would be allowed to learn to canoe. A camper would go out into the lake with a counselor, and once the counselor felt that the boy had mastered canoeing, the canoe would be capsized and the counselor would swim back to shore. It was the responsibility of the camper to retrieve the paddles and return the canoe to shore. Once the camper could do this, he or she was allowed to take the canoe out on their own. After meals, campers were required to take an hour's rest in their cabins. Naps, stories from counselors, letters home and reading occurred during rest time.

Campers were instructed in all sports. The camp advertised the new sport of "aquaplaning" or "water tobogganing." Aquaplaning was a sport that developed around 1909–10 as boat shows participants attempted to ride a toboggan or ironing board–shaped plank of wood while being towed by a boat. Boats, often called launches at the time, had just become powerful enough to tow a rider. Aquaplaning was the first towed watersport. The challenge in riding was to stand upright on the board without being tossed overboard. The sport became popularized after Theodore Wallis invited the editors of *Outing Magazine* to Camp Mishe Mokwa to demonstrate the sport. Wallis indicated that aquaplaning was "a game that gives all the fun of flying without the danger or the cost."

The "plane" was a five-by-two-and-a-half-foot wooden board based on Hawaiian surfboards. It was built using several "ordinary boards and fastening them together by three cross boards or cleats." Once assembled, the board was painted with white lead and finished with a coat of marine paint or varnish. A three-quarter-inch tow rope was attached at the upper corners, spliced to screen door handles. The plane was attached to the boat, and the boat began to move at a slow pace as the rider reached the rear of the board. The rider would lie flat on the board as the boat picked up speed. Riders would ride the board as you would a kneeboard, getting into a standing position on the board once the boat reached a speed of about twenty miles per hour. Wallis and the campers of Mishe Mokwa demonstrated their teaching strategies and aquaplaning prowess to the editors of *Outing Magazine*, effectively teaching a novice rider to aquaplane within a few hours. Aquaplaning continued as a sport at Mishe Mokwa during its duration as a camp on the lake. Tandem riding, cross riding, shoulder carries and other variations were the goals of the campers. Jumps were added as a common stunt. The sport itself continued into the 1950s until it fell out of favor for waterskiing, which had been invented in Minnesota in 1922.

Demonstration of the sport of aquaplaning at Camp Miske Mokwa for the editors of *Outing Magazine* in 1914. *Courtesy of Archive.org.*

Excursions from Camp Mishe Mokwa included a day trip to Portsmouth to deep sea fish for cod, and once a summer, the boys at the camp would have the opportunity to ride the *Mount Washington* around Lake Winnipesaukee. An overnight hike and camping trip to Mount Chocorua also occurred once a summer. Campers at the camp would sleep in bungalows with open sides and sloped roofs. Each bungalow had six cots down on each side and would sleep twelve campers. After supper, campers would lounge on the veranda of the lodge and sing around the piano, play card games or take evening canoeing trips around the island. As dusk settled, blankets were grabbed from cabins, and campers settled around the campfire for an interesting story. As soon as the story ended, campers would retire to their cabins as taps was played.

An infirmary was built on the island opposite the docks and shoreline. The camp infirmary was staffed with a full-time physician. In 1924, the camp had an outbreak of mumps, and campers were quarantined until the disease ran its course. A one-hundred-foot artesian well was installed into bedrock and provided fresh running water to the camp. The camp had flush toilets and a full septic system.

Many of the counselors at the camp were Dartmouth, Yale and Harvard students. Young men were exposed to Yale football from the number of counselors from the Yale football team, including Raymond "Ducky" Pond, who went on to coach football at Yale; Phil Bunnell, captain of the Yale football team in the mid-1920s; Yale tight end Stuart Scott; and Yale football team manager Charlie Williamson. Football drills were common in the fields and around the cabins of the camp.

During the summer of 1924, two sea planes landed in the channel between Treasure Island and Smalls Cove and taxied up to the camp docks. Pilots offered up flights for four or five dollars for a ten-minute trip around the lake. The short flight was the highlight of many campers' summers. Will Horner's boat, the *Brookline*, was for hire for fishing trips in the early 1900s and was a popular excursion boat for the summer camps in the area.

The campers participated in an Inter-Camp Photographic Contest hosted by A.H. Beardsley and *Photo Era Magazine*. The contestants came from various Winnipesaukee camps, including Camp Mishe Mokwa in West Alton, Camp Kuwiyan in East Alton, Camp Kehonka in Alton and Camp Owais'sa and Camp Wyanoke in Wolfeboro. Directors and counselors were barred from entering the contest. The emphasis of the photograph submissions was on flora and fauna, portraits of fellow campers and camp views. Campers were taught rudimentary photographic composition about foreground, placement of subject in the photo, horizon lines, distortion of portraits, focusing and over- and under-exposure. Campers were awarded engraved silver bowls for first, second and third place and honorable mentions. The silver bowls were paid for by the directors of the five participating camps. The winning photographs were placed on public display and printed in the fall issue of *Photo Era Magazine*. Judges of the contest included "three qualified" individuals with no ties to any of the summer camps. During the 1924 contest, Mishe Mokwa campers Herman Liebert, Frank Bowditch and Hebert S. Wallis earned honorable mentions for their photographs titled *Lake, Mountain and Forest*, *Top of Mount Major* and *Put It Over*, respectively. The following year, additional lectures on photography were given by outside speakers who showed examples of what to do and what to not to do. Campers showed increased knowledge of the art of photography during the second year of the contest with the increased instruction.

Mishe Mokwa operated as a boy's camp between 1913 and 1937, when the Depression took its toll on the camp and the island was foreclosed on. The camp was reopened during the summer of 1940 on the Clark Pond tract, owned by Dartmouth College in Canaan, New Hampshire.

Camp Treasure Island

In 1938, Treasure and Cub Islands were sold to the Girl Scouts of Boston, and the camp was rebranded as a Girl Scout camp, Camp Treasure Island. Just as the Girl Scouts took ownership of islands, the Great New England Hurricane hit the Winnipesaukee region. The Girl Scouts held a rummage sale at Horticultural Hall to raise the funds to rebuild the camp.

Girl Scouts and Girl Guides from across the globe would attend Camp Treasure Island, some traveling from Scotland and Canada to attend the camp on Lake Winnipesaukee. Girls would travel by train from North Station in Boston to Dover, New Hampshire. Girls would then get on a Laconia bus to Colby's Inn at Smiths Point in West Alton, where they would be loaded onto the *Bunny*, a white Chris Craft that had a capacity of up to thirty campers. The camp had four sessions of two weeks each.

In 1949, as campership grew, the camp realized that it would need a second boat. The campers planned to raise the funds to purchase one. Using funds from the annual Girl Scout cookie sale and the rummage sale, Troop 104 of South Boston attended an auction of surplus material at the Boston Navy Yard. During the auction, they found out that they could be gifted a boat from the navy, but it would need to be through an act of Congress. In 1950, Congress approved the gift of the gray navy double-ended surplus whaler. The launching was a gala event on Lake Winnipesaukee. Everyone who had a hand in the acquisition was invited in addition to local lake residents, congressmen and representatives of the U.S. Navy. Troop 104 had the honor of christening the boat. A breakaway bottle was used to break over the bow, and gray balloons were released. The *Cookie* made its maiden voyage to the camp on Winnipesaukee on July 23, 1950. If rain was in the forecast, the campers would be transported in *Bunny*, and their bedrolls and

Two Girl Scouts peeking out of a tent while on an overnight camping excursion at Camp Treasure Island. *Courtesy of Lake Winnipesaukee Historical Society.*

duffels would be transported in *Cookie*. A small outboard was used for daily food runs and taking counselors back and forth to the mainland for time off.

Each unit in the camp had two cabins that housed four to six campers and a small cabin for two counselors. The units included Crow's Nest, Fiddlers Green, Topmast and Cub. Girls cooked in outdoor kitchens with cinderblock charcoal grills for breakfast and lunch. Campers would transport food from the main lodge, the Anchor Inn, to their individual units in wicker backpacks. Dinner was held in the main lodge, one of the few buildings on the island that had electricity and contained a large pantry and a commercial kitchen. At night, the camp was lit using kerosene lanterns. Campers cut firewood from dead wood found around the islands. Girls were instructed in all manner of

Girl Scout campers arrive at Camp Treasure Island on the *Cookie*. *Courtesy of Girl Scout Museum at Cedar Hill.*

Boating captain and a new round of Girl Scout campers arrive at Camp Treasure Island. *Courtesy of Girl Scout Museum at Cedar Hill.*

cooking from how and what kindling to gather, the type of fire they needed and various cooking devices such as a reflector oven—skills that Girl Scouts are still learning at camp today, as noted in the 1929 Girl Scout handbook:

> *One glance at a camper's fire tells what kind of woodman he is. It is quite impossible to prepare a good meal over a heap of smoking chunks, a fierce blaze or a great bed of coals that will warp iron and melt everything else. If one would have good meals cooked out of doors, and would save much time and vexation; in other words, if he wants to be comfortable in the woods, he must learn how to produce at will either (1) a quick, hot, little fire that will boil water in a jiffy, and will soon burn down to embers that are not too ardent for frying; or (2) a glowing smokeless heat for baking, roasting, or slow boiling; or (3) a big log fire that will throw its heat forward on the ground, and into a tent or lean-to and will last for hours without replenishing.*

Wartime meat rationing continued through 1946, but poultry was not rationed. The camp went through fifteen turkeys per week. Campers ate turkey meat, turkey soup and turkey every which way six days a week. Fridays were always macaroni and cheese nights. The camp hosted an annual barbecue each summer at camp. Everyone who served the camp—from the butcher, the baker, the mailman and all others involved in the service of the camp—was invited.

Just as with Mishe Mokwa, the majority of the activities revolved around the waterfront. Girls were issued a swim test on their first waterfront session, just as they are at Girl Scout camp today. The swim test consisted of a demonstration of floating for one minute or treading water for one minute, a demonstration of swimming one stroke for one hundred yards and a demonstration of two separate strokes. Girls could go on to earn their swimming badge if they also demonstrated the ability to recover themselves after falling into the water; the standing front dive or racing start from the shoreline dive into the water; being able to swim twenty yards in seventeen seconds using the crawl or trudgen crawl; and a demonstration of the ability to play three water games such as cross tag, volleyball, tug of war and dodge ball. Water polo, basketball and baseball were considered too strenuous for water activity. Girls should be able to demonstrate the Schafer method of resuscitation. The Schafer method has the victim or patient lying prone on their side, with the rescuers' knees straddling them as the rescuer exerts pressure on the back at a rate of twelve compressions per minute. Finally, girls needed to know the precautions they should take when swimming

Girl Scout campers cooking breakfast or lunch over an open fire grill at Camp Treasure Island. *Courtesy of Lake Winnipesaukee Historical Society.*

in unfamiliar waters. After passing all those tests, they would earn their swimming badge.

Originally, the camp had no shore power. Electricity was generated by a Delco unit running a generator. The Anchor Inn, the dining hall and kitchen had lights powered by the generator. Several strands of lights were strung through trees but were uninsulated and were shut down in rainstorms. Refrigeration came from ice cut from the lake in winter and stored in the icehouse with sawdust insulation. Ice was taken from the icebox to the kitchen as needed. Ivar Swenson, of Sleepers Island, engineered a power cable for Treasure Island. After the cable was installed, Ivar was made an honorary Girl Scout. Campers would row twelve-person canoes to the castle on Sleepers Island and would play all day with all the fun items and crafts that were kept in the barn at the castle. There was also a working piano with many music paper rolls. One of the campers' favorite songs was an Eskimo love song, "Oogi, Oogi, Wa Wa":

"Oogi Oogi Wa Wa" (1922)
Lyrics by Grant Clarke and Edgar Leslie. Music by Archie Gottler.

Where it's Zero, all the year-o
Lives an Eskimo

He looks funny with his honey
Sittin' in the snow
They're a happy couple
All dress'd up in furs
Warm as an oven, while they are lovin'
Here's what occurs

[Chorus]
He sighs and whispers
Oogie oogie wa wa, Oogie oogie wa wa
She sighs and answers
Oogie oogie wa wa, too
Don't that sound absurd, just a crazy word
It don't mean much to you I know
But it means an awful lot to an Eskimo
And oh! Boy! they love that
Oogie oogie wa wa, Oogie oogie wa wa
It makes a person curious to know
But you'll get fooled, just the way I was
'Cause the word don't mean what you think it does
Oogie oogie wa wa means I wanna Mama
To an Eskimo

It's all snow there still men go there
Find the pole and then
For some reason ev'ry season
They go back again
Yet these same explorers
Often lose their way
While they are tramping
Maybe the vamping leads them astray

[Chorus]
He sighs and whispers
Oogie oogie wa wa, Oogie oogie wa wa
She sighs and answers
Oogie oogie wa wa, too
Girls like simple things

Beads and ten cent rings
They kiss you for a choc'late drop
Just imagine if a fellow had a candy shop
And oh! Boy! they'll holler
Oogie oogie wa wa, Oogie oogie wa wa
They live the life of Riley don't you know
Imagine women, wine and song
On a night up there that is six months long
Oogie oogie wa wa it's nice to be the Papa
Of an Eskimo

The campers would travel all around the southern end of the lake by canoe. Trips to Weirs Beach, Wolfeboro and Alton Bay were not uncommon. Girls would canoe from island to island. Former campers remember visiting Stonedam Island, Camp Idlewilde and Long and Cow Islands. Longer excursions to the White Mountains included a week camping trip to the Peabody Slopes on Cannon Mountain and exploring the Flume Gorge

Girl Scout campers swimming at Camp Treasure Island. *Courtesy of Girl Scout Museum at Cedar Hill.*

Girl Scout campers performing a swim test at Camp Treasure Island. *Courtesy of Lake Winnipesaukee Historical Society.*

Girl Scout campers swimming at Camp Treasure Island. *Courtesy of Lake Winnipesaukee Historical Society.*

at Franconia Notch. Campers would go overnight camping on several of the islands, including Sleepers, Diamond and Rattlesnake. During trips to Rattlesnake Island, the girls cleared the initial trails around the island and to the summit. Longer day-hikes were conducted to Mount Major and Mount Chocorua. The girls sang taps every night as the flag was lowered and folded. Mail was delivered by the mail boat in Alton Bay. On Sundays, the boat would come to the camp and take the Catholic girls across the lake to church in Wolfeboro.

Older girls would stay in the unit on Cub Island. Girls would paddle over from Cub to Treasure for activities and paddle back to their unit for meals and rest. Sailing to Ship Island was not uncommon.

Treasure Island Poem
Unknown Author

Treasure Island grew here when the world was still quite young.
God carved it with His glacier and set it in the sun.
He poured out lake around it, and sheltered it with care,
Then covered it with rocks and trees to make it green and fair.
But when this work was finished, God couldn't leave it so—
His masterpiece of beauty, and no one here knows.
He thought of all the centuries it would stand here all alone,
So He gave it a loving spirit, just for its very own.
And down through all the ages, this spirit has guarded our isle,
And the beauty of all she's seen here is reflected in her smile.
She remembers the sweetness of springtime, the feel of the south winds warm,
The cold of a thousand winters, and the power of a storm.
All these are remembered, and these she will tell you.
If you just sit and listen, and let her voice come through.
If ever you want to hear her, just listen to the breeze,
As it whispers of the days gone by among the old pine trees
Or sit at night by your campfire, when the embers have burned down low,
And she will tell of other nights, and their Indian fires' glow.
What, have you never seen her? Just stand at Golden Gate,
And watch the setting sun go down in a haze across the state.
Or spend the night at Topmast, and you'll see her golden hair.
As the moon shines through the branches of the 3 grey birches there.
And so when we must leave here, our sadness of farewell
Is lessened because we understand the spirit remains to dwell.

Girl Scouts hauling a canoe on to the shore at Camp Treasure Island. *Courtesy of the Lake Winnipesaukee Historical Society.*

> *She will guard our treasured island, through all the winter long.*
> *She'll wait, and watch, and remember, and tell it to us in song.*

The flag was required to be raised just after sunrise and retired at sunset. The flag would not be raised during stormy days or left out overnight, except during wartime. The blue field should be facing east toward the rising sun. A flag ceremony would start and end the girls' day. Girls would sing patriotic songs such as "The Star-Spangled Banner," the hymn "America" and "The Battle Hymn of the Republic" and recite the Pledge of Allegiance. Girls were instructed in folding and unfolding a flag, and each unit or patrol would take a turn at leading a flag ceremony. At today's Girl Scout camps, similar structure occurs with the flag ceremony, but units would lead additional camp songs and skits after the traditional patriotic songs and hymns were sung. Taps would close out the flag ceremony at night:

> *Day is done, gone the sun,*
> *From the lake, from the hills, from the sky;*
> *All is well, safely rest,*
> *God is nigh.*

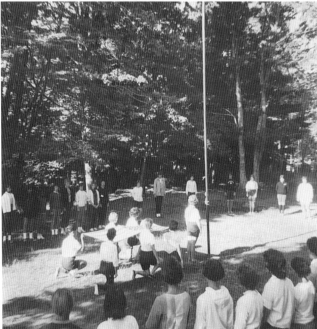

Above: Girl Scouts performing a flag ceremony at Camp treasure Island. *Courtesy of Girl Scout Museum at Cedar Hill.*

Left: Girl Scouts performing a flag ceremony at Camp Treasure Island. *Courtesy of Lake Winnipesaukee Historical Society.*

The Boston Girl Scout Council owned and operated Camp Treasure Island until 1964. Costs to run the camp were increasing, and the Girl Scouts did not want to pass the increased increase costs off to the campers by increasing camper fees. Camp Treasure Island had its last camper during the summer of 1963.

Vacation Home Era

The Boston Girl Scout Council sold the island to Willetts and Forrest Manchester of Canton, Massachusetts, in 1965. The Manchesters developed a subdivision plan for the island that consisted of seventeen shorefront lots. The Treasure Island Boatel was opened the same year in order to entice buyers to the island. Boatels had become popular in the 1950s, and one existed on Sleepers Island during the same time. The Treasure Island boatel advertised cabin camps and tent sites available for the season, month or week. Hot showers, electricity, canoes and rowboats and a water ski school were among the amenities. The Treasure Island boatel, like the Sleepers Island boatel, was short-lived, and by 1968, lots began to be sold off on the island for development into vacation home properties. Several of the original Mishe Mokwa and Camp Treasure Island cabins still exist on the island today.

SHIP ISLAND AND MOOSE ISLAND

Moose and Ship Islands are located southeast of Rattlesnake Island in Alton, New Hampshire. Moose Island is the larger of the two islands, comprising 1.5 acres. Ship Island is 0.17 acres in comparison. Both islands rise to an elevation of 502 feet above msl, or 2 feet below average lake level. The two islands are in the outer part of the Belknap Complex Ring Intrusion and are the remnants of an old caldera of a volcano that formed during the breakup of the supercontinent Pangea. Moose Island is labeled as Varney's Island on the 1881 Boston and Maine Railroad Map of Lake Winnipeseogee and Vicinity.

Moose Island was purchased in 1922 by Harry Perkins (see the "Fisherville" section), Edwin K. Jenkins, H.S. Clark, A.S. Jenkins and John and Charles Proctor in an equal one-fifth partnership. The island was owned by the five parties for their natural lives.

Ship Island was owned by Stinson L. Taylor, an executive with the New Hampshire Petroleum Industries Committee. Taylor served as the state petroleum administrator under the National Recovery Act, chairman of the New Hampshire Highway Users Conference and president of the New Hampshire Good Roads Association. He was a navy veteran of World War I and a member of the state Fire Control board. He gained the reputation for being the "watchdog" of the highway department. In 1954, the Stinsons sold the island to Eliot Umberto Wyman, a Wolfeboro lawyer.

Eliot Wyman was on the town council and on the Wolfeboro Budget committee. The Wymans owned several properties throughout Wolfeboro, including one off Springfield Point, the Jesse Whitten Lot and a property on North Main Street formerly owned by the Goodhues. They also owned property nearby Red Hill in Moultonborough and Brookfield, New Hampshire.

The Wymans owned the island for eleven years before selling it to William Belanger of Brookline, Massachusetts. The extreme island life proved too much for Belanger, and he sold the island the following year to Robert Kayser Jr. The Kaysers would own the island for nine years before selling it to Norman and Alice Schmidt of Harvard, Massachusetts. The Schmidts owned Ship for twenty-six years and sold the island and all the property contained within it to the Audesse family of Dunbarton, New Hampshire, in 2001. In 2011, the island was sold to its current owners, the Konings.

There have been several shipwrecks off the shores of Ship and Moose Islands. Two wrecks are located off the eastern shoreline of Ship Island. The first wreck is a 1950s-era twenty-five-foot closed-bow cruiser. The second wreck is located to the north of the first wreck in about eighty-five feet of water. The deeper wreck is an eighteen-foot red-hulled boat with white decking and a steering wheel. A motor, shaft and batteries can be seen in the shallower wreck. Scuba divers frequently anchor off Ship Island to investigate these two wrecks. A shallow shoal exists around the islands, causing a navigation hazard for boaters. The prevailing northwest wind across the islands can be fierce, with little to block the wind as it travels across the Broads.

Moose Island contains six individual property lots ranging in size from 0.1 acres to 0.6 acres; however, two of those lots cannot be built on. Ship Island contains only one private parcel. Neither island has electric service; electricity is generated by propane, which is delivered by barge to the islands.

THE ISLANDS OF ALTON BAY
AND EAST ALTON

The wind shifted to the north-northeast and blew a gale, scattering the clouds, and by the time our steamer passed out of the bay into the lake, the water was white-capped, and waves broke heavily on the small islands, flinging their foam and spray against the green foliage on the shores.
—John Greenleaf Whittier

LITTLE MARK ISLAND

Little Mark Island is 0.20 acres in size and is located at the mouth of Alton Bay. The maximum elevation of the island is 502 feet above mean sea level or 2 feet below average lake levels. It is a navigational aid on the lake. A lit buoy was added near Little Lark Island in 1930.

During a storm in 1880, the *Winnipesaukee*, which was carting an excursion party from Alton Bay, started to break up just beyond Little Mark Island. It was a frightful experience for the passengers and resulted in the beginning of the present-day legislation for the inspection of public boats.

The first owner of record was J.H. Burtt, a Boston merchant in 1895. The island was sold to Charles Dore sometime after 1895. The island was sold upon Charles's death in 1916 to Herman A. Perkins. The purchase of the island included a naphtha launch, all furnishings, a cottage and a boathouse. Perkins would only own the island until 1923, when it was sold to Lucy Ellen (Read) Nute. The island was sold in 1942 to Arthur and Barbara Smith.

Photo postcard of Little Mark Island, circa 1910. *Courtesy of author.*

Photo postcard of Little Mark Island with Mount Major in the background. *Courtesy of author.*

The Smiths sold the island because their kids thought it was like living on Alcatraz. A priest named Father Frederick J. Hobbs purchased the property from them in 1953 after he retired. Father Hobbs was a Roman Catholic priest who attended seminary at St. John's Seminary in Brighton in 1929.

His younger sister Louise Hobbs had a cottage in Young's Cove. Little Mark Island also had a parcel of land on Woodlands Road. It was used as a staging area and launch for construction materials and supplies for the island. After Father Hobbs passed on, the property and Little Mark was sold to the Brooks family.

In 2009, a snowmobiler broke through the ice in the waters near Little Mark. The rider struggled in the waters for fifteen minutes before he was able to pull himself out. He hiked over the ice to Little Mark Island and took refuge for the night in an unlocked cabin. In 2011, the island and the land were put up for auction, and each was purchased by separate individuals. The mainland property was acquired by an abutter to expand his existing lot, and the island was acquired by a second entity. After years of the structures being unoccupied, the elements took their toll on Little Mark. In 2022, the structures on the island were leveled. Construction on a new structure began in the spring of 2023.

WOODMAN'S COVE ISLANDS

Two small islands are located in Woodman Cove in Alton Bay. Woodman's Cove Island is a 0.1-acre islet formerly known as Canney's Island. Mount Major Island is 0.18 acres. The two islands were originally included as part of mainland shore property.

Woodman Cove is named for Jeremiah Woodman. Jeremiah was a private in Captain Nathan Brown's Company in Colonel Piere Long's Regiment of the New Hampshire Line during the Revolutionary War. He enlisted in Poplin and served from August 1776 through August 1777. Jeremiah came to Alton and acquired a tract of wild land three miles northwest of the village. He married Sarah Chase of Barnstead, New Hampshire.

The islands of Woodman Cove were two of the unnumbered islands on the Masonian grant and included in the sale from the Sanders heirs to attorney Fullerton Wells in 1915. The first owner of record after Wells was Andrew J. Ward of Alton, New Hampshire. Ward owned six separate parcels of land in the Woodman Cove area. He leased 1.5 acres of one of the parcels to the Winnipesaukee Yacht Club, 6 acres to the Lake Shore Railroad and 1.5 acres to the Cape Pond Ice Company. The six parcels were acquired by Ward between 1892 and 1900 from various owners.

Between 1889 and 1930, the Lake Shore Railroad operated the Mount Major train stop at Woodman Cove.

By 1907, a clubhouse of the Winnipesaukee Yacht Club was located just north of Woodman Cove. The yacht club was organized in 1903. The club's headquarters was originally located on Sandy Island, with a second location proposed on Little Bear Island in Tuftonboro. The yacht club was focused on the encouragement of water sports, seamanship and navigation; proper buoying and lighting of the lake; protection of fisheries; protection from pollution; and the welfare of the lake. As membership of the club grew, the club looked to construct clubhouses to represent the various areas of the lake. Lakeshore Park in Gilford, Melvin Village and Wolfeboro were looked at as possible locations for additional clubhouses. The yacht club began hosting a series of powerboat races in 1904, with one class for sailing boats and two for motorboats. A location in Alton Bay was selected as one of the additional clubhouses in 1907. The yacht club was a large wooden building with a large wraparound porch. The interior of the building was a large thirty-by-thirty-foot room that was used in the winter to store the club's sailboat. Dances were held in the clubhouse during the week, and a balcony over the front door was where the orchestra sat during the dances. A long dock was built on the property, and boat races were held around the cove islands.

On May 16, 1921, ownership of Mount Major Island, Woodman Cove Island, the Winnipesaukee Yacht Club parcel and six mainland parcels in the Woodman Cove area were sold to Frank Herman Hilton. The Winnipesaukee Yacht Club was open until 1928. At this time, the islands and the clubhouse were broken into small parcels of land for sale.

Hilton in turn sold Mount Major Island to Harlow Harris Halliday in June 1929. The island remained in the Halliday family, passing through heirs to Leone Halliday Sias Hulse, who sold the island in 1968 to Leonard Brown. The Brown family occupied the island for three decades, selling the island to current owners Anne and Norman MacInnis in 1996.

PLUM ISLAND AND QUARTER-MILE ISLAND

Plum Island, formerly known as Half-Mile Island, is a 1.5-acre islet in Roberts Cove, Alton, New Hampshire. The island was originally owned by Sewell Roberts of Roberts Cove. A smaller vacant island located close to the shoreline is known as Quarter-Mile Island or Mystery Island. Quarter-Mile Island is a 0.12-acre islet located 237 feet from the mainland shore. In 1894, this island was sold by Isaac Leighton Stockbridge to Sewall Roberts. Stockbridge was a cooper and stone layer in Alton. The Roberts family were one of the founding families of Alton (New Durham Gore). Joseph Roberts Moved from Portsmouth to New Durham, New Hampshire, in 1792. Four years later, New Durham was split into New Durham and New Durham Gore. Upon arrival, Joseph, his wife and their son Richard began cultivating a large tract of land. He built a log cabin on the land; his great-grandson Sewall Edson and Ella Trask Roberts would later live in the original log cabin. Sewell and Ella inherited the Alton farm in 1883. At the time, the farm comprised 350 acres.

Quarter-Mile and Half Mile Island remained in the Roberts family until 1928. Quarter-Mile became part of the real estate transactions for land

Photo postcard of the Alton shoreline, circa 1910–20. *Courtesy of author.*

Left: Sailing in Alton Bay, Alton, New Hampshire, date unknown. *Courtesy of author.*

Below: Photo postcard of Roberts Cove, Quarter Mile Island (formerly Mystery) and Plum Island (formerly Half-Mile) in the background. *Courtesy of author.*

on Roberts Cove and has been included in the property transaction of the mainland property since then. The Roberts family sold Plum Island to Harrison Brown of Rye, New Hampshire, on August 27, 1927. Plum Island passed through Harrison Brown to his daughter Marjorie Miller and her son Timothy Miller before being sold to Christian Camps and Conferences Inc. (Camp Brookwoods and Camp Deer Run) in Alton, New Hampshire. The area around Plum Island is a common loon nesting location, and a floating loon nest was installed in the waters around Plum Island by the Loon Preservation Society of Moultonborough.

THE BARNDOOR ISLANDS

The Barndoor Islands were included in Lot No. 1 of the Masonian grant along with Sleepers Island, the eastern portion of Rattlesnake Island and Diamond Island. Lot No. 1 was granted to Tomlinson and March.

Joseph Varney purchased four islands in Wolfeboro Harbor in 1809. These four islands were identified as Barndoor Islands in Lot No. 1 of the Mason Grant and included the islands of Barndoor, Little Barndoor, Keniston and Melody. In 1799, these four islands fell under the jurisdiction of Alton, New Hampshire. In 1896, Big and Little Barndoor were officially made Alton islands, and Keniston and Melody were annexed to Wolfeboro.

An urban legend states that the gap between Big and Little Barndoor appeared to be a barn door when viewed in the right light and angle and during the right time of day. The barn door held the two islands together by its hinges. The barn door that appeared was a trick of the light off the water. The mainland barn no longer remains, but the name has stuck for the two Alton islands. Big Barndoor Island is about eighty-eight acres, while Little Barndoor comprises just over five acres and resides within the boundaries of the town of Alton.

The islands are located in Alton, New Hampshire. Barndoor Island is eighty-eight acres of predominantly level topography. Barndoor has a maximum elevation of 515 feet above msl, or 11 feet above mean lake levels, while Little Barndoor has a maximum elevation of 509 feet above msl, or 5 feet above mean lake level. Eighteen acres in the center of Barndoor Island are conserved common land for shoreline properties. The common area is surrounded by an old construction road that was used to develop the island.

Photo postcard showing the gap through the Barn Doors. *Courtesy of author.*

BIG BARNDOOR ISLAND

In the late 1920s, Ralph George Carpenter Jr. of Boston, Massachusetts, and Wolfeboro, New Hampshire, owned a summer home on Barndoor Island. Carpenter was the grandson of George Carpenter of Wolfeboro, for whom the Carpenter School is named.

Mr. Carpenter worked as an agent for the New Hampshire Fish and Game Department. Carpenter owned the Barndoor Island Game Preserve. Charles Roberts, son of Sewall Roberts (of Roberts Cove), built the original barn on the property from timber harvested on the island for Carpenter. Carpenter built a large barn on the island for the dairy cows he kept on the island. Oxen would be used to haul hay over the ice to the island.

George Carpenter also raised and trained carrier pigeons. While a student at Harvard, he owned a gray goshawk and was experienced in the sport of falconry. On October 19, 1931, six carrier pigeons were transported to the Blake Building in Boston, Massachusetts, which housed the real estate office of his grandfather. Messages with the time of release were strapped to the pigeons' legs, as well as other data about the birds. The pigeons had previously completed several shorter test flights to deliver the news of a baby's birth from Rochester, New Hampshire, to Barndoor Island. The Rochester

Harry Perkins (1869–1959) and
Sherman Adams (1899–1986) in 1958.
Courtesy of Wolfeboro Historical Society.

to Barndoor flight was completed in twenty-two minutes by the pigeons. The pigeons were released from the rooftop of the Blake building at 10:30 a.m. for their one-hundred-mile flight.

In later years, two white-tailed deer became a part of the preserve. These deer were named Flagg and Bucky, and in the 1940s, Carpenter transported them to the annual New England Sportsman show with several wild game such as ducks and geese that made their home on the island. The wild game were placed on exhibit for all the area hunters visiting the show. The Barndoor game preserve contained numerous types of wild birds, fowl, fancy hens, pheasants, elk, sheep and goats in addition to the homing pigeons. Later in 1939, a beaver family was relocated from Errol to Barndoor Island for the purpose of observation and scientific monitoring. Ralph Carpenter went on to become the director of New Hampshire Fish and Game and received an honorary Doctor of Science degree for his work with fish and game.

FISHERVILLE

The waters around the Barndoor Islands were well known for their fishing hot spots, and in the wintertime, when the lake freezes over, a transient city called "Fisherville" would spring up. Harry "Whiskers" Perkins was the honorary "Mayor of Fisherville" and would maroon himself on Barndoor Island until the ice froze over and the fishing huts popped up. Perkins would work as a caretaker for Carpenter's game preserve and assisted in the transport of the animals across the ice to the New England Sportsman's show. Perkins would stay at the show and answer inquiries about ice fishing on Winnipesaukee before returning to the lake with the wild game. Harry Perkins held Fishing License no. 1 for several years and was the authority on where to fish in Winnipesaukee.

A newly caught fish is being measured to see if the catch is legal at the Fisherville Municipal Court, Wolfeboro, circa 1940. *Courtesy of Wolfeboro Historical Society.*

Fisherville was originally founded in 1888 several hundred yards off the shore of the Wolfeboro Town Docks. In 1940, the transient town of Fisherville was incorporated under the New Hampshire secretary of state under the direction of Ralph G. Carpenter II. As an incorporated city, Fisherville contained a city hall, a city hall annex, a city library, a city jail, a municipal courthouse, the Last-Chance Saloon, the Fisherville Square Garden and a newspaper called the *Fisherville News*. The city of Fisherville was divided into six precincts, each with a "Precinct Boss." Residents of Fisherville arrived by airplane, ice boat, automobile, skates, skis and on horseback.

Fisherville had a tradition of recycling the town's Christmas trees into the Fisherville Municipal Forest. Fisherville residents would collect the Christmas trees from the streets around Wolfeboro. The trees were lined on both sides of the Smith River channel to create the forest. Fisherville City Hall was described as the town's most pretentious building and was constructed with a tiled fireplace, wood floors and running water. A cupola and a fisherman's weathervane graced the roof of the structure; the latter had a cusk on one end and a "tommy cod" on the other.

Ralph George Carpenter Sr. (1885–1963), Charles Glidden (1926–2004), "Mayor" Harry Perkins (1869–1959) and Warren Smith (1912–1977) in front of Fisherville City Hall in 1940. *Courtesy of Wolfeboro Historical Society.*

In 1942, the Municipal Power and Light Company added steeplejacks to the city of Fisherville and illuminated the winter city for the first time. The city hall in later years added an antenna, generator and telephone to the building.

Fisherville disbanded as an incorporated city in the late 1950s, and by the 1960s, the founding town members no longer resided in Fisherville during the winter season. Harry Perkins had moved into an assisted living facility and passed away in 1969 and was buried at the Jones Wildlife Management Area in Middleton, New Hampshire.

VACATION HOME ERA

After twenty-five years as the director of the New Hampshire Fish and Game, Carpenter retired. The Carpenters sold their Barndoor Island property in 1966 and moved to a one-thousand-acre ranch, the Lazy AA, in Casino Creek, Montana, and built a winter home on mainland Winnipesaukee.

The island was sold to three parties: David Cohen, Murray Nussinow and Robert Ronci. The trio formed Barndoor Associates for the purpose of subdividing the island. In 1969, a subdivision plan was approved for the island. The island was divided into seventy-one shoreland private lots and one interior lot. A launch from the Wolfeboro Inn operated at the hour to bring potential owners out to see the lots on Barndoor Island. The launch operated on the hour Friday, Saturday and Sunday. In 1978, the interior lot was sold to the newly formed Barndoor Island Association. A 1.5-mile-perimeter walking trail is located on the common interior land owned by the association for island residents to enjoy.

LITTLE BARNDOOR ISLAND

We set sail again to a point off Little Barndoor Island where we can command an unobstructed view of the main lake as far as the eye can reach. The wind has died out completely. We shut off the engine and drift lazily as we wait for the grand symphony of color in the western sky. Soon a heavy bank of clouds in the west becomes brilliantly illuminated with the rays of the sinking sun.
—*A.H. Beardsley, 1921*

Little Barndoor Island is located north of Big Barndoor and has an unobstructed view of the main lake. It was formerly known as Baker Island.

The first owners of record for Little Barndoor are William C. Thomson and William Fox of Wolfeboro. Fox and Thomson were lawyers in Wolfeboro and provided many mortgages for properties around Wolfeboro and the surrounding towns. Little Barndoor was annexed from Wolfeboro to Alton in 1897, Wolfeboro obtained Melody, Keniston, Church and Littlest Mud Islands, and Alton received the islands of Barndoor and Little Barndoor. In 1899, the island consisted of two parcels. The first parcel, owned by Fox and Thompson, was sold to Blake Folsom in 1899. The second half was sold by Charles and Ida Piper to Folsom three years later in 1902.

The Folsom family was another of Wolfeboro's original settlers. Blake Folsom operated dairy farm and owned the local hardware store in Wolfeboro. Upon Blake Folsom's death in 1911, Little Barndoor was bequeathed to Orville Porter.

Orville Porter sold the island in its entirety to Curtis Dickens in 1915. Orville had come into possession of the island through the death of his

Wolfeboro, N. H. A Bit of Barn Door Island

Photo postcard titled "A Bit of Barndoor" from the Wolfeboro shoreline. *Courtesy of author.*

uncle. Dickens owned the island until August 17, 1945, when he sold it to Arnold and Beatrice Osterlund Jr. All furniture, furnishings and the thirty-foot powerboat *Kathyrn* were included in the sale. The Osterlunds purchased Little Barndoor for $5,000.

Arnold Osterlund Jr., of Plainfield, New Jersey, was a civil engineer and private pilot. On September 24, 1960, Osterlund took off from Laconia airport in a Cessna 172 bound for his primary residence in New Jersey. His plane went down over Pack Monadnock in Temple, New Hampshire.

Following the death of Arnold, Beatrice sold the island to Carl and Helen VanWinckel Sr. The VanWinckels transferred the island to their son, who sold it in 1969 to Holly Porter in Grand Rapids, Michigan. Porter later sold the island to Michigan-based Barndoor Associates. Barndoor Associates, however, never developed the island, and in 1977, it sold the island to Clarence and Anna M. Pierce of Lynn, Massachusetts. In 1982, the Pierces developed the subdivision plan for the island and began to sell off six individual lots for summer home properties.

In 1980, Barndoor and Little Barndoor Island achieved stardom in the film *On Golden Pond*. While the majority of the filming for the movie was completed at neighboring Squam Lake, the Barndoor Islands were the backdrop of several boating scenes in the movie. Residents remember waking up to the sound of a helicopter over the island, and initial speculation was that a police chase was occurring. However, the helicopter remained "chasing" the boat for hours, and it soon became obvious that this was for other purposes. It wasn't until the movie came out that residents learned of the filming around their islands.

PARKER ISLAND

Roughest spot with the highest waves in a northwester is Parker Island…Unlike the immense swells of the sea, though, the waves on the lake are nearer together and more sharply pointed. Every fifth wave there is a lull. In this calm the wise lake navigator makes his turns and course changes.
—Paul Blaisdell, 1938

Parker Island is a five-acre islet in Wolfeboro, New Hampshire, located between Wolfeboro Neck and Rattlesnake Island. It rises to an elevation of 505 feet above msl, or 1 foot above average lake levels. Parker Island is named for John Parker, one of the original Wolfeboro town proprietors who owned about six hundred acres on Wolfeboro Neck. Parker Island is a navigational landmark on the lake and the first island encountered on an approach to Wolfeboro Harbor from the Broads.

Surveyor Walter Bryant estimated that Wolfeboro neck contained 1,200 acres and divided it into two lots, which were drawn by Henry Rust and John Parker. When the actual survey was conducted, it was found that Wolfeboro Neck only contained 567 acres. This tract was granted to John Parker, and Henry Rust was allowed to take 600 acres from the "Bryant Reservation." John Parker became the clerk of the newly organized township. In 1711, John Parker was made sheriff of the province. As the population of the province grew, it was divided into counties, and Parker was appointed sheriff of Rockingham County, the most populous county. As a federal government was being formed, he later was appointed marshal of the district of New Hampshire. He held these offices until his death in 1791.

The first owner on record of the island is David W. Fullerton. On May 13, 1874, the island was sold to William J. Fox and Daniel Horne for one dollar. William Fox also may have owned Melody Island at this time. William Fox was a local lawyer and was effusive in his prose. His deed transfers read like poems:

> *Know all men, Lords, equires and peasants*
> *And know all women by these presents—*
> *In short let all creation know,*
> *That I Bill Fox of Wolfeboro*
> *State of New Hampshire, County Carroll,*
> *A yeoman bald, unused to hair oil,*
> *In duplicate consideration*
> *Of good will towards my blood relation,*
> *And two Bears feet most oleaginous*
> *(Ungrateful let no man imagine us)*
> *To me in hand before editing*
> *Or ever thought of was this writing*
> *(And which I, bound for land o'Canaan,*
> *Will daily rub upon my cranium)*
> *Delivered by one Witt D Carter*
> *A true descended Son of Sparta,*
> *And ward (a) ad litem of old Nimrod,*
> *The Tutelar saint of gun and ramrod*
> *Of Ossipee in State Affiresaid,*
> *And County ditto (be no more said*
> *Of that (b) venue for tattlers gossipy.*
> *Enough will tell of "righteous" Ossipee)*
> *Do thus remise, release and quitclaim*

Excerpt from deed of Ossipee Mountain from William Fox to Witt De Carter, 1866. However, it should be noted that Fox had no claim to the property he transferred to his friend Witt, and Witt never acted on the land transfer despite it being recorded in the Carroll Country Registry of Deeds.

The pair owned the island for seven years, after which William Fox sold his share to Horne, making Horne the sole owner of the island. Horne developed the island property, and in 1886, Horne's "Parker Island House" was the "best appointed island house in the entire region." The Parker Island House soon had frequent summer visitors, especially those who liked to fish. The Parker Island House was described as a "miniature hotel with everything in apple pie order for the accommodation of its delighted guests." It was available for any guests who were staying at Horne's on the Lake (Belvue House/Lake Shore House) on Wolfeboro Neck. The steamer *Spray* was purchased in July 1897 from the Libby brothers' sawmill in Wolfeboro. The *Spray* had been used by the Libby brothers to tow logs to their sawmill. Horne would use the steamer for excursions in and around the lake and often carried guests from the Belvue/Lake Shore House to Parker Island.

Horne operated the *Spray* until 1899, when he sold it to Willis E. Tetherly. Tetherly continued to allow the *Spray* to be used for charters from the Belvue/Lake Shore House to the Parker Island House in the subsequent years.

On June 1, 1898, Horne's on the Lake and the Parker Island House were leased to Frank P. Hobbs. Hobbs took title to the mainland property on August 5, 1901, but soon ran into financial difficulties and went bankrupt in 1903. During this time, Parker Island and the mainland property were no longer connected in use, and the island ceased to be an excursion for guests of the hotel. The Belvue/Lake Shore House was razed in 1940. Frank Hobbs also owned the docks behind the Peavey Block and allowed public use. He cautioned the public to restrict their time at the docks to short errands and passengers picking up and dropping off when the docks were busy.

One Sunday afternoon in July 1890, Mrs. and Mrs. Horace Pope, the owners of the Pleasant Point Cottages in Alton, and a group of friends and relatives boarded the twenty-eight-foot steamer *Irene* for an excursion around the lake. Suddenly, a storm arose, and the waves increased. The *Irene* put in at Parker Island, and the excursionists sought refuge in the Parker Island House, entering by taking a door off its hinges. A sign reading "REPORT IRENE SAFE ALTON BAY" was made using blueberry juice from the ripe berries on the island and a bed sheet. Passengers on the *Mount Washington* saw the sign and reported to anxious families in Alton Bay that everyone on the *Irene* was safe at Parker Island.

Parker Island passed to Dan Horne's heirs for several generations. The Parker Island House became the family camp, and the island was used privately by the Horne family and their friends until 1930. On August 27, 1930, William B. Hone and his sister Marian B. Sias sold the island to Willian and Margaret H. Underhill. The Underhills only owned the island for three months when it was sold to Hilda H. Hopewell. Hopewell owned a summer estate on Tips Cove in Wolfeboro. The island at this time contained a small wooden dock and two buildings on the southwestern shore. An outhouse was located toward the center of the island. One of the buildings had a piano, and power was supplied to the buildings through an on-site generator. The Hopewells used the island for picnics and camping parties, using their mainland property for lodging.

On September 1, 1957, Homer Cotton and three other men were boating for Wolfeboro Harbor when they were caught in a wind and rainstorm. The group sought refuge on Parker Island, just as the earlier group on the *Irene* did. Six-foot waves had pushed Cotton's boat toward the rocky shore of Parker Island, and his engine cut out. The following morning, they signaled Louis Wyman at his summer home on Wolfeboro Neck. Wyman called Nat Goodhue to rescue the group.

The island was transferred to Hopewell's three sons—Harry, Robert and Frank—on May 16, 1960. The Hopewell brothers owned the island until 1967, when it was sold to James and Natalie Locke of Barnstead, New Hampshire. The Lockes divided the island into two parcels and sold the other half to Robert and Priscilla Dustin. In June of the same year, both halves of the island were sold to Beverly Moseley and P&F Enterprises. The following year, the island transferred ownership again to the American Land Development Corporation for $15,000.

Don Storms ("Diamond Don"), CEO of Amway, owned it and called the island Storms Island. Don was a Christian gospel singer with the group The Envoys, host of the Christian television show *More than Music* and owner of C&S Builders. Parker Island is currently divided into two private summer home properties.

WORCESTER ISLAND

Worcester Island is one of six bridged islands on Lake Winnipesaukee. It comprises twenty acres and rises to an elevation of 522 feet above msl, or 18 feet above average lake levels.

The first record of ownership of this island belongs to Samuel Avery. Samuel married Mary Moody Clark, and they made their home in Wolfeboro in 1814. Samuel was involved in blacksmithing, shoemaking, harness making, milling, coopering and farming. At one point in his business dealings, Samuel ran the woolen mill with Nathaniel Rogers and Daniel Pickering until a fire consumed the business. It is unknown when the island came into Samuel's hands, but it was bequeathed to his sons Joseph and Augustine in 1858. Augustine held many positions in Wolfeboro from town clerk to treasurer and was representative for the town for three years. Augustine and Joseph married two Libby sisters. Augustine married Sarah Libby and had five children; the eldest son, Dudley Libby Avery, lost his life to drowning in the lake on June 24, 1874, at the age of seventeen.

Joseph and his wife sold their half interest in Worcester Island, a mainland parcel and Tuftonboro island Little Bear Island in 1888 for $1,000 to his brother Augustine. In subsequent years, the three parcels were broken up in separate real estate transactions. The island was sold to Allison E. Rines, who sold the island to Dorothea and Samuel Hunt in 1935. The Hunts would go on to sell the island to Joseph Melanson of Wolfeboro.

In 1949, Melanson (see Rattlesnake Island) purchased the island for $2,700. He did not hold on to it for very long before selling it a year later to Fred E.

Three girls canoeing in Lake Winnipesaukee, date unknown. *Courtesy of author.*

Varney and Gordon Colby. Varney and Colby also purchased a mainland lot on Springfield Point. Varney, the owner of Fred E. Varney Construction and chairman of Wolfeboro Sewer department in the public works, began road construction through the point to Worcester Island. Gordon Colby was a supervisor in a construction company. In 1955, Fred Varney and Gordon Colby paid to have the Municipal Electric Company of Wolfeboro and New England Telephone and Telegraph extend the electric and telephone service to the island. Varney was the water and sewer commissioner for the Town of Wolfeboro.

In 1967, a subdivision plan was approved for Worcester Island, and the island was subdivided into fourteen individual shoreland lots. Construction of the lots was completed by Varney and Colby. During a drought year, the water was low enough that a bulldozer was able to create breakwaters and beaches, which would not have been possible otherwise.

THE VARNEY ISLANDS

The Varney Islands—formerly also known as the Fisher Islands and Small Mud Islands—comprise more than twenty islands off Wolfeboro Harbor. The islands are located between Worcester Island and Springfield Point in South Wolfeboro and Barndoor Island in Alton, New Hampshire. Eleven of these islands—Harmony, Gate, Shelter, Little Keniston I and II, Blueberry, Keel, Scavenger, Winch, Overnight (Nostab) and Cove Islands—are vacant. The name is derived from the Varney family of Wolfeboro.

The Varney Islands are relatively flat in topography or described as a pile of rocks and shrubs. On average they rise to an elevation of 502 feet above mean sea level or 2 feet below mean lake levels.

COLONIAL SETTLERS

Joseph Varney bought four large islands identified as Barndoor Islands in Lot No. 1 of the Mason patent in Wolfeboro Harbor. These islands were formerly a part of Alton, New Hampshire, when Joseph Varney purchased them in 1809. The islands had been annexed in 1799 to Alton, in whose jurisdiction they would stay for the next century. These islands, though not identified by name, were identified by their acreage and included Barndoor, Little Barndoor, Keniston and Melody Islands.

Sometime before 1812, the remaining unnumbered islands on the lake were acquired by Samuel Abbott of Tuftonboro. Abbott was one of the original colonial settlers in Tuftonboro. In 1812, he sold the islands to Josiah Sawyer, a blacksmith in Tuftonboro for forty dollars. At Sawyer's death in 1850, the islands were sold by the administrator of his estate to four Gilford men—Thomas Plummer, John Thyng, John Potter and John Plummer—for a sum of fifty-five dollars. The four men owned the islands for five years before selling them to George Goss and Henry Doan of Gilford for sixty dollars. Doan soon bought out Goss's share in the islands. In 1858, Abraham Morrison of Gilford acquired them, and six years later they were sold to George Sanders, a lumberman of Gilford in 1864.

George Sanders at this time also owned a four-hundred-acre farm on the mainland in Gilford, as well as Round and Timber Island. Sanders used the islands as a source of lumber for his lumber yard in Gilford. Sanders owned the unnumbered islands until his death in December 1903 while ice fishing at his Glendale camp. The islands' ownership transferred to the Sanders heirs Joseph S. and J. Frank Sanders. J. Frank Sanders later sold the islands to Fullerton Wells, a New York lawyer, who formed the Lake Winnipesaukee Islands Company in 1912. The deed of transfer identified 212 islands. The islands not included in the Wells land deal included Black Cat, Beaver, Hull, Three-Mile, Pine, Bear, Five-Mile, Six-Mile, Follette, Smiths, Mark, Mink, Timber, Governors, Pitchwood, Locker, Welch, Jolly, Birch, Nine-Acre, Chases, Farm, Dows, Whortleberry, Rock, Long, Little Bear, Cow, Sandy, Rattlesnake, Sleepers, Barndoor, Little Barndoor, Keniston, Barneys and Stonedam. Over the previous century, several of the unnumbered islands transferred ownership through "adverse possession" or "squatters rights." Squatters rights allow an individual to claim ownership of a property if they have occupied it without the consent of an owner, demonstrated that they were living there (built a structure, logging the property), did not hide their presence and stayed on the island for at least twenty years. Most were unoccupied, were too small and had little value in the pre–summer home era. Several found value in their use as fishing camps. By the mid-1800s, many of these unnumbered islands were being used as fishing camps for avid fishermen of the area. Black, Diamond, Badger, Whaleback, Worcester, Ganzy, Glines, Poplar, Half-Mile and Mile Islands were the islands identified as the most prominent islands in the land transfer of the unnumbered islands to Wells.

Wells engaged a Tilton, New Hampshire news agency photographer to photograph all the islands in his purchase and create postcards of them to advertise them for sale. Many of the early postcards of the islands came about due to his marketing. His intent was to convert the islands into New York residence colonies. He incorporated the Winnipesaukee Company and invested $25,000 for his endeavor. Wells was a well-known New York attorney and used his connections to market the islands for a profit. Wells became a founding partner in Robbins and Wells in Long Island and specialized in real estate law. He passed away on October 17, 1959.

Lewando and Tilton on the Peavey Block in Wolfeboro made deliveries of groceries and general merchandise by boat to the Varney Islands between 1890 and 1914.

KENISTON ISLAND

Keniston Island was formerly known as Waveland Island and Baker Island. It is the largest of the Varney Islands named for Joseph Keniston. Joseph Keniston was an early Wolfeboro settler. He was a Revolutionary War soldier and farmer. Keniston Island reaches 560 feet in elevation above msl, or 56 feet above average lake levels. It is 17.02 acres in size. The island is separated from Melody Island by a channel. Keniston Island was the first of the Varney Islands to be built on.

In 1899, a group of prominent Lynn, Massachusetts citizens purchased Keniston Island from Mary A. Warren. Lynn city solicitor Stan Parsons, engineer Fred H. Eastman and Lynn city claim agent Fred A. Broad formed Waveland Improvement Association, purchased the island for one dollar and renamed it Waveland Island. The Lynn group quickly sought to divide the island into thirty-seven house lots and sold several lots within the first year to fellow Lynn residents. Arrangements were made for the construction of a larger landing at the island for regular day trips between the island and Wolfeboro harbor by steamer. Some of the first purchasers were other prominent Lynn, Massachusetts citizens such as Harold Valpey and Lynn city engineer Smith.

Lumber was transported over the ice during the winter to be ready for building out the first lots in the spring. The Lynn group secured local contractor J.A. McCathern to erect the cottages on the newly purchased lots. Local carpenters traveled to the island for the building, and seven thousand bricks were shipped from the Lynn area to the island for chimneys and fireplaces in the cottages. The group advertised the great fishing off the island and organized a fishing excursion to entire other local Lynn families to purchase a lot on the island.

The Lynn residents pooled their money and purchased a steamboat that they christened *Waveland*. The boat was stored in a boathouse on the common waterfront lot for the island. The *Uncle Sam* mail boat initiated regular stops on the island on July 1, 1909. The island escaped much of the damage from the 1938 hurricane, with reports of electric wires holding the trees off from hitting cottages. Later in the 1990s, the Wolfeboro mail boat *Blue Ghost* took over mail service for the residents of Keniston. The name Waveland was primarily used for the island through the 1910s and 1920s and then sporadically throughout the remainder of the twentieth century. The island is now solely known as Keniston Island.

MELODY ISLAND AND THE NEW HAMPSHIRE MUSIC FESTIVAL

Within the next two weeks, people living in and around Wolfeboro points blessed with unusual natural acoustics will be hearing faint notes of flutes, oboes, trumpets, violins and cellos. Folks skimming gaily over Lake Winnipesaukee in their boats will hear not only the delightful sounds, but also, if you circle around, the dramatic chords and arpeggios of piano concerti and instrumental chorus of a complete orchestra rehearing. The source of this enchantment as nearly everyone in this region knows is Melody Island.
—Granite State News, *June 22, 1956*

Melody Island—formerly Varney Island No. 1, Browns Island and Big Mud Island—is an eighteen-acre island in Wolfeboro, New Hampshire. It rises to an elevation of 515 feet above msl, or 11 feet above mean lake levels. Town records include the acreage of Harmony Island in the total acreage of Melody Island. The island is irregular in shape with a cove on its northwest shore, facing Wolfeboro Harbor. During low water times, Harmony Island is a small rock peninsula to Melody Island. The vacant Harmony Island is included in one of the private home lot (Lot No. 22) on Melody Island. Melody Island is one of the four islands annexed from Alton to Wolfeboro in 1897, and early records for these islands can be found in Town of Alton and Belknap County files.

The first record of ownership after Joseph Varney is that of David C. Rogers. Rogers at the time seems to have acquired "ownership" of several islands in the area through squatters rights. Rogers indicates that Melody (Mud Island) and the small islands immediately surrounding it, known as the "Small Mud Islands," were never occupied for cultivation, wood or timber logging or occupied with a tenement in his deed transfer. In 1878, he sold Melody Islands and the surrounding smaller islands that are now known as Church and Littlest Mud to William Fox and a lawyer in Wolfeboro and to Burt Carter, also of Wolfeboro. Fox and Carter paid $200 for the collection of islands.

The duo owned the islands jointly for seven years, when Carter sold his half of the islands to William's wife for $150. The pair had only sold off one lot on Melody Island, in the northwestern corner of the island facing Wolfeboro Harbor. This lot was sold to Freeman Johnson, who began developing his lot. By 1896, William C. Fox was working with a crew on Melody Island, cutting timber. Ice had formed around the island less than one hundred feet from the shore, so a channel was kept open to get the boat in and out with the timber. Mr. Fox would later meet his demise on the shores of Melody Island. While on a fishing trip with his son, William drowned off shore of Melody on May 21, 1897. His son was able to reach the shore after their boat capsized, but his father never did. His body was recovered the following day. Ownership of the islands transferred to William's wife, Lizzie.

In 1920, the only structure on the island was an old boathouse of indeterminate age that was located in the cove facing Wolfeboro Harbor. On July 4, 1930, the *Granite State News* advertised the northwestern point (Freeman Johnson property) of Mud Island for sale. The parcel was described as containing 1.25 acres and as a "good location for a camp." The parcel was purchased by George S. Casebolt, a Harvard student, under Arthur W. Hanson. Hanson was the father of Robert Hanson, who went on to purchase many of the Varney Islands. During this time, Lizzie Fox began to sell off the individual islands surrounding Melody. E.M. Fifield of Medford, Massachusetts, purchased the remainder of Mud Island on December 2, 1938, and planned to develop the island.

The hurricane of 1938 did not spare the island. The *Granite State News* reported on December 2, 1939, "Mr. Fifield of Medford, Massachusetts, has a problem righting his boathouse which was turned topsy turvy during the September hurricane." In 1940, a boathouse was rebuilt on the east side of the island, with a cabin about fifty yards to the northwest of the boathouse.

In 1946, concert pianist and piano teacher Madame Hedy (Hedwig) Spielter and French actor Jules Epailly purchased "Mudd Island/Varney Island No. 1" and the surrounding small islands then known as the Small Varney Islands/Small Mudd Islands. The purchase excluded the Casebolt property on the northwestern corner. Spielter and Epailly renamed the island Melody Island in their musical pursuits and developed the property as a musical summer camp. Epailly and Spielter first built a large building and brought several spinets and large upright pianos to the island. The camp contained a boathouse, sixteen or more bunkhouses (ten-by-ten-foot structures) and a combination mess hall and music building.

Hedy is described as a stout woman who enjoyed old-fashioned clothing and wore her gray hair in a bun. She studied piano first with her father, Hermann Spielter, and later studied piano and composition in France with Isidor Philipp, Camille Decreus and André Bloch at the Fontainebleau Conservatory in Paris. When she returned to the United States, she was awarded a scholarship to Juilliard and was instructed in music composition by Rubin Goldmark. Hedy was an aspiring concert pianist when she injured her wrist on a rough weather trip returning from Germany in 1928. She fell down the stairs on the steamboat *Stuttgart* and sustained a Colles fracture to her left wrist, a concussion and a two-inch laceration on her head in addition to other bumps and bruises. Hedy indicated that the ship failed to rope off dangerous parts of the ship while in rough weather and filed a $75,000 suit against the steamboat company, North German Lloyd Steamship Company. After her injury, Hedy was unable to continue performances and shifted her focus to the teaching of other promising young pianists. The original verdict that found in favor of the steamboat company was overturned after jurors came forward indicating that they had been "browbeaten and bulldozed" into a verdict for the defendant, who was a claims adjuster for the shipping companies. Hedy received a new trial, but the original verdict was upheld, finding in support of the steamship company.

Jules Epailly was a French actor who had spent twenty-five years on Broadway before partnering with Hedy to teach music. Jules was known as a violin virtuoso. His career as a musician was ended when he suffered a hand injury fighting with French forces during World War I. Epailly last appeared on Broadway in 1940. His most recognizable film roles were beside Bob Hope in *Going Spanish*, in *Follow the Leader* and as a Frenchman in *Gentlemen Prefer Blondes*.

Spielter opened the Melody Island School of Music on the island to continue teaching piano as she summered on the lake. She did not believe in rest, so in order to continue her teaching and her students' training, she would often bring many of her New York students with her to study on the island. Camper fees were $500 for July 1 through September 1 and included studies in piano, orchestra, composition and harmony. There was no age limit, and Hedy accepted coed students. Initially, the Melody Island School of Music had a few cabins for students, a small swimming beach, one boat and a few canoes. The main house was the former owner's cottage. Spielter and Epailly cleared the middle of the island, built an amphitheater and made room for boaters to dock on the shore. They began hosting concerts and recitals for their students. Several students performed local recitals in Wolfeboro during their summer training.

After summering for several years on the island, the couple sought to bring orchestral music to the lakes region and provide their students with the opportunity to perform with professional musicians. The first concert series was held in 1953 and included performances from students at the Melody Island School of Music and Spielter's protégés. Concerts were given twice a week throughout August.

Soloists included Stecher and Horowitz, dueling pianists; solo pianists Leonor Umstead, Sheila Minzer, Alan Mandel, Ellen Stern and Barbara Berkman; violinists Willy Frey and Joseph Pepper; violist Morris Shostock; flutist Phillip Dunigan; and oboist Marilyn Miller. As a result of the success of the concerts, Spielter and Epailly, along with Maurice Bonney, the conductor of the New York Symphony Orchestra, formed the nonprofit group Friends of the New Hampshire Music Festival in 1953. The New Hampshire Music Festival performed concerts in the lakes region and surrounding towns, holding several on the island. The concert season ran from July 1 to September 1, with the final concert of the season always held on Melody Island. Locals could attend the concerts by boat or ride island taxi boats leaving from the Wolfeboro docks. The Melody Island boat *Go-Go* was a narrow cabin cruiser. Nat Goodhue attempted to maintain it for the island, but the *Go-Go* was "sunk more than it was afloat." Nat Goodhue would take the *Swallow* out and anchor off the shore of the island to listen to the concerts with the other islanders and locals. It is reported that Nat would delight in teasing Epailly by refusing to call the island "Melody," instead favoring its original Mud Island name. Nat Goodhue and the *Swallow* would assist in the transport of concert goers from the Wolfeboro docks to Melody Island for the concerts.

Students who trained under Spielter at Melody Lake had the opportunity to rehearse and play with a forty-piece orchestra and appear as soloists in concerts in the surrounding communities. The first year, the organization was fully funded by Spielter and Epailly. The pair offered sponsorships the following year to offset their costs. More than six hundred people purchased sponsorships. The pair would go on to expand the amphitheater and build a wooden band shell on the island that could hold up to three hundred guests. During the summer of 1953, several concerts were presented under the Amy Cheney Beach Club, a local group that was dedicated to music appreciation. The group, under the direction of Ella Lord Gilbert, took interest in Madame Spielter and her students and supported her cause of furthering music education and appreciation. The first concert under the auspice of the Amy Cheney Beach Club was held on Monday, July 20, and included a picnic supper. The patrons were ferried by Captain Nat Goodhue on the *Swallow* from the Wolfeboro Town Docks. The band shell was packed. In the opening chords of Beethoven's *Symphony No. 8*, the clouds opened, and a downpour of rain fell on the concert and its patrons. The musicians finished the symphony, and the rest of the concert was canceled and rescheduled for the following Friday evening. The Friday concert included numbers such as Schubert's *Symphony No. 5*.

The Melody Island Music School originally only had instruction in piano, music theory, harmony and composition. Additional training in other instruments was added to the school as interest grew with professional and amateur musicians. The festival drew prominent musicians from around the United States. Melody Island was dubbed "Little Tanglewood." The New Hampshire Music Festival gained so much popularity that concerts began to be held not only on the island but on the mainland as well. In 1955, the schedule for concerts was modified to include concerts in Gilford and Wolfeboro. Estimates had more than two thousand people attending New Hampshire Music Festival concerts by the third week in July. The island primarily housed the musicians, students and practices spaces and a handful of concerts.

Conductor Leopold Stokowski and his family spent ten days on Melody Island with his family. Upon leaving, he indicated that he had been impressed with two piano students and felt that they had talent in the highest order, as well as with the program of symphony music from all periods. Stokowski went on to invite several of the students to perform with him in Houston the following year and made a donation to further support the music festival. Maurice Bonney retained the title of music director for the festival, but his new position as associate conductor of the Houston Symphony did not allow for him to be present during July 1956. This allowed Dean Ryan, founder and conductor of the Academy of Chamber Players of New York, to conduct the festival in his absence. WMUR-TV presented a feature on Melody Island during the summer of 1956.

During the week, students on Melody Island could be seen on the island relaxing while listening to chamber music or playing chess. The summer of 1956 saw about forty-three musicians in residence, and finances were increasing with the increased attention to the camp. The music festival had grown so large that it outgrew Melody Island. One of the musicians was Yvonne Bizet, granddaughter of the French composer Georges Bizet, and she noted, "This is a paradise for us! Musicians are always so tired. Here we can relax completely!"

Chamber music concerts were presented for free on the island every Sunday evening during the 1956 season. An additional nine adult concerts and two children's concerts were performed on the mainland. By the summer of 1959, the New Hampshire Music Festival was operating at a loss and could no longer afford to host concerts on the island. The headquarters of the festival was relocated to the four-story Garnet Inn in Centre Harbor. All the concerts were moved off the island. The New Hampshire Music Festival found a new home at Plymouth State University at the Silver Center for the Arts Plymouth, New Hampshire, and is celebrating its seventy-first season of summer concerts.

Upon Hedy's death, Jules Epailly sold Melody Island and the surrounding smaller islands to S&B Realty on September 14, 1961, which created the Melody Island Associates. Melody Island Associates began to divest the islands into eighteen smaller vacation home lots. The New Hampshire Music Festival continues to draw world-class musicians and conductors from across the globe, but concerts on the island ceased in 1961.

Church Island

Church Island was formerly known as Little Mud Island. It is the largest of the "Small Mud Islands" and is the third-largest Varney Island at 3.8 acres. Little Mud was originally included in the purchases of Melody Island (then Mid Island) until 1936. In 1936, Ellen Stokes sold Church Island to Hebert and Vivian Walker of Evansville, Indiana, for fifty dollars. Ellen was the daughter of William and Lizzie Fox. The Walkers built the cottage that resides on the island today. They owned the island for twenty-five years

Melody Island development flyer, circa 1962. *Courtesy of author.*

before selling it to Arthur and Mary Agnew in 1961. In 1966, the island was sold finally to the McNitt family, who also purchased Spider Island (Walker Island). The McNitt family continue to own the island today.

Previous records have indicated that Little Mud Island was also owned by the St. Andrews Episcopal Church in New Jersey. However, no ownership records have been found to confirm the church's ownership history. The ownership provenance contains no gaps from 1878 to the present time. It is likely that *Littlest* Mud should have the "Church" moniker, not Little Mud.

LITTLEST MUD ISLAND

Littlest Mud Island was formerly known as Dr. Smith Island and Varney Island No. 2. Littlest Mud Island was earlier deeded as part of Little Mud Island. The two islands form at high water. Littlest was named by Jacob Peter Den Hartog since it was the smaller part of Little Mud Island. Littlest Mud Island is 1.5 acres and has a maximum elevation of 502 feet above msl, or 2 feet below average lake levels. In the late nineteenth century, the islands were named the Dr. Smith Islands for Dr. Jeremiah Ranlett Smith.

Dr. Smith was a surgeon and Civil War veteran. Immediately after mustering out of the Civil War, he opened a medical practice in Wolfeboro, where he practiced medicine for five years. In 1870, he moved his primary residence and practice to Gloucester, Massachusetts. As his health started to decline, he retired and returned to Wolfeboro in 1891. In 1897, Smith's Island was annexed from Alton to Wolfeboro with Keniston, Melody and Church Island.

In 1901, the islands transferred from Emma J. Smith and the estate of her father, Jeremiah Ranlett Smith, to Charles W. Hoyt, a Wolfeboro carpenter. Hoyt paid ninety dollars for the island. Myra L. Beacham a

Wolfeboro milliner, and Cora M. Thompson purchased the island from Hoyt in 1904. The pair owned the islands for a decade before selling it to Florence H. Whitman. Florence and Raymond Whitman owned the island until 1923, when it was conveyed to Charles H. Wells. Wells left the island to the St. Andrews Church in his will. At some point, the island came under the ownership of Ralph Carpenter Jr. (see "Barndoor Islands" chapter). Carpenter sold the islands to the Hartog family in early 1938.

J.P. and Elisabeth Den Hartog arrived in Wolfeboro every weekend to oversee construction of their cottage on Little Mud. J.P. was a professor at Harvard. He enlisted in the U.S. Navy during World War II and rose to the rank of captain in the Naval Reserve. After World War II, J.P. went to teach at MIT for the next twenty-five years. The Hartog family entertained foreign scientists at their cottage on Littlest Mud. The family owned Little Mud Island between 1938 and 2011. Thomas Bell purchased the island from the Hartog estate and subsequently built two new cabins on the property—a sleeping cabin on the water's edge and a one-bedroom cabin with a kitchenette and three-fourth bath.

GRANT ISLAND

Somewhat rough and rocky on that aquatic place called Winnipisseogee.
—David "Farmer" Rogers, 1877

Grant Island, formerly known as Fisher Island and Coffin Island, is a small island north of Worcester Island and Springfield Point. The island is close to the mainland shore near Canopache Road in South Wolfeboro. The island covers 0.321 acres and rises to an elevation of 502 feet above msl, or 2 feet below the average lake elevation.

The island was originally listed as Coffin Island, named for Stephen Coffin, who moved from Alton to Wolfeboro to a farm in South Wolfeboro. It can be assumed that Coffin owned the mainland farm adjacent to the island. Stephen Coffin was the son of Jonathan Coffin and Jane Flanders Brown (see "Sleepers Island" chapter). Stephen was a clergyman and led churches in both Alton and later in life Dover, New Hampshire. Stephen and Deborah had only one son, Lorenzo S., who went on to follow in his father's footsteps as a reverend in Iowa. Stephen died of "disease of prostate gland" in 1868 at the age of seventy-five.

On March 10, 1877, David Charles Rogers sold the island to O. Merrill Fisher, a traveling salesman from Montpelier, Vermont, for five dollars. David Rogers was known locally as "Farmer Rogers" and was the son of Nathaniel Rogers and Martha Rust (see "Rattlesnake Island" chapter). David married Sarah Elizabeth Clark of Wolfeboro in 1850. Together they had five children: Charles Henry, Ellen Florence, Nathaniel, Herbert Eugene and one other who was unnamed. Rogers was also active in the state legislature, much as his father and grandfather were. He was a delegate to constitutional conventions for "Wolfeborough and Classed Towns" from 1861 to 1862 and from 1867 to 1868.

The deed for Grant Island was written by Rogers and William Fox (see "Parker Island" chapter) during a fishing trip. Rogers, however, did not have legal possession of Coffin Island. The island at this time had not been charted, and no one ever had legal possession of it. Fox indicated that Fisher "looked his name." Rogers blessed the land transfer of the island with the following: "From Fisher Island may the Fish-House rise, its fish browned smokestack pierce the lucky skies, its walls be cheered with ever happy faces, and all our fish lines fall in pleasant places." In the deed, the pair changed the name of the island from Coffin to Fisher Island—"let the name of Coffin buried be, and Fisher stand while rivers seek the sea"—in honor of the new owner and his appropriate name. Mr. Fisher had the deed recorded, and as no one could produce a title to the island, he became the first official owner of the island.

In 1892, O.M. Fisher deeded the island to the Grant family and Henry H. Chase for one dollar. Continuing the tradition granted to Fisher, the island was renamed Grant Island for its new owners. The island is now named Grant Island for Lorenzo Trafton Grant, who was born in Lyman, Maine. Grant enlisted as a private in the 9th Maine Infantry Regiment for the Union army in 1964. He joined the regiment with the Army of the Potomac at Gloucester Point, Virginia. Lorenzo, the 9th Maine Infantry Regiment and the Army of the Potomac sailed and participated in action at Drewry's Bluff, Bermuda Hundred and Cold Harbor and the capture of Fort Fisher in North Carolina. While part of the Army of the Potomac, the regiment took possession of Wilmington and joined General Sherman's forces at Cox Bridge, where the group continued to Raleigh, North Carolina. Grant remained in Raleigh through July 1965, after which the regiment was sent home to Maine. Grant mustered out with the rest of the regiment after a year in service.

Sometime in the decade between 1870 and 1880, Grant moved to Wolfeboro, New Hampshire. Upon arriving, he worked as a stage driver and stable keeper. In 1897, he contracted malaria and passed away. The island passed to Lorenzo's wife, Mary S. Grant, and then to his son Charles R. Grant. The Grants and Henry Chase co-owed the island until 1922, when Chase deeded his half to the Grants.

The Grant family continued to own the island for several more years. However, in 1928, they sold the island to Joseph Goodwin Jr. for the sum of one dollar. Joseph was the son of Joseph and Ellen (Furber) Goodwin of Wolfeboro. Joseph was a lawyer for Crawford, Harris & Goodwin in Manhattan, New York. Joseph married Elizabeth Lester Jones of Richmond Hill in 1913.

The Goodwins spent many of their summers at the "Fish-House," as it was called back then. It is unknown whether this was in reference to the Fishers or to its use as a fishing camp. The Fish-House was furnished with a kerosene stove, an icebox, Morris chairs, a bed and a fireplace. The

Vacationers arriving at the "fish camp" on Grant Island, Wolfeboro, unknown date. *Courtesy of Wolfeboro Historical Society.*

Goodwins and their heirs owned Grant Island until 1971. In 1954, the deed to the island was transferred to Joseph and Elizabeth's grand-nephew, John Ordman of New York City. John Ordman was the son of Dr. Charles W. Ordman and Elizabeth Goodwin of Washington, D.C. Elizabeth was the daughter of Joseph's brother, Elisha Goodwin of Boston. John Ordman owned the island for the next twenty-three years before selling it to Robert and Nancy Stephenson in 1971. Robert (Bob) Stephenson began summering in Wolfeboro in 1946. He was the grandson of Dr. Nathaniel Scott. Scott owned a home on Pickering Street where he practiced, now known as the Scott House. The Stephensons purchased a mainland home, Cove-Camp, on Stephenson Lane and Scott Road at the same time as they purchased Grant Island.

The following year, the cover of the annual edition of the New England Telephone Company directory featured a sunset over Grant Island. Over the next years, the Fish-House would deteriorate, and in 2007, a new summer home was built in its place.

BLUEBERRY ISLAND

Blueberry Island is a small island off Keniston Island, 0.25 acres in size. It was formerly known as Little Keniston Island. In 1970, Bob Hanson was checking on bringing electrical service from Keniston to Blueberry Island. He observed that Blueberry Island was mismarked on the town map and began to inquire on the ownership of all the small Varney Islands. After further research, he found that they were still included in the original deed for Melody Island. At the time, William Sweeney, who owned Melody, was unaware that he was also the owner of all the other small islands surrounding Melody. Bob Hanson and William Sweeney struck up a deal to purchase the small islands. Chip and Winch were retained by Armin Langsten, who helped broker the deal. The names Chip Island and Winch Island were named by Langsten's two sons, Jon and Michael, and were officially recorded as the official island name. The island has mail service by the *Blue Ghost* mail boat out of Wolfeboro.

UPPER SHOE ISLAND

Upper Shoe Island is a 0.22-acre islet located northeast of Melody Island. Maps and historical documents have spelled Upper Shoe in various methods, from "Uppershoe" to "Uppeshou"; however, Upper Shoe is the official island name as of 1993. Upper Shoe has a one bedroom, off-the-grid cottage on the island. It has been said to have been given the name by Professor Jacob Pieter Den Hartog, who took the name from an old sign circa 1940 after finding a magazine at the camp. In 1897, it was one of four islands (Keniston, Melody, Upper Shore and Church Islands) annexed from Alton to Wolfeboro. The island has been occupied as early as 1907. In 1908, Charles Hoyt sold the island to J. Wilbur Tilton, a Wolfeboro merchant. Tilton owned the island for eleven years before it was sold to Dr. Myron Davis of Ossipee. In 1938, it was purchased by Dr. J.P. Den Hartog and his wife in addition to Little Mud and Littlest Mud.

SPIDER ISLAND

Spider Island was formerly known as Walker Island. Spider is a one-acre island that contains a two-bedroom, one-bath cottage on it. It was originally named for Dr. Hebert Walker and his wife, Vivian, who owned it in the 1930s; it has two cabins and a boat storage shed. In the 1930s, there was no electrical service to the island, and the owners used an evaporative cooler to preserve food.

CHIP ISLAND

Chip Island is a 0.3-acre islet located to the west of Littlest Mud Island. A one-story cottage was built on the island in 1982 by the Langsten family, who also own Winch Island. The Langstons named the island after their thirty-foot Catalina sailboat *Blue Chip*. They additionally have a dinghy named *Chippy*.

VACANT VARNEY ISLANDS

The remainder thirteen Varney Islands are owned by five separate parties and are vacant land. The majority of these islands were named by the current property owner or their family members. These islands were included in descriptions of the Small Mud Islands, which were also formerly known as the Small Varney Islands.

Little Keniston Island I and Little Keniston II are located just off the east-southeast shoreline of Keniston Island. Little Keniston I is an 0.8-acre islet, while Little Keniston II is a 0.1-acre islet. The two islands are currently owned by the Town of Wolfeboro.

Lone Pine Island was formerly known as Babson Island II. Lone Pine Island is 0.28 acre and located between the mainland shore and Spider Island. The Lone Pine name was made official on July 6, 1994, by town selectmen—one can suspect due to a single lone pine on the island.

Harbour Island is a 0.25-acre islet located off the shore of the small bay on the northwest side of Melody. It is described as "rocks with bushes and trees." It is named for nearby Harbor Bay but was given the British spelling.

Gate Island is a 0.2-acre islet located off the shore of Melody Island. It was most recently known as one of the Small Melody Islands and included in the deed for Melody Island. It is described in town records as a rock with bushes. A shallow rock reef extends between Church Island and Gate Island. The island was named because it makes an effective barrier to navigation except for a small opening or gate.

Winch Island is a 0.02-acre islet located 250 feet from Shelter Island. It was named for the winch on a sailboat.

Overnight Island was formerly listed as Babson Island and Nosbab Island ("Babson" backward). Overnight Island is a 0.11-acre islet, located east of Spider Island, between Spider and the mainland shore. A small, unnamed island, it's more of a pile of rocks, located just off its northeast shore. The Overnight name was made official on July 6, 1994, by town selectmen.

Scavenger Island is a 0.02-acre islet, southeast of Church Island and west of Winch Island. The owners' sons used to dive off the rocks and scavenge for treasures such as fishing lures and anchors, hence the name.

Shelter Island is a 0.01-acre islet that was mostly recently known as one of the small Melody Islands and was included in the deed for Melody Island. Shelter is located on the lee (east) side of Melody Island. It is sheltered from the wind and waves.

Keel Island is a 0.08-acre islet most recently known as one of the small Melody Islands and included in the deed for Melody Island. It is located southeast of Church Island and west of Winch Island.

Ledge Island is a 0.11-acre islet. It is located to the east-southeast of Keniston Island and northeast of Spider Island.

Jib Island is a 0.29-acre islet and one of the former Small Melody Islands. It is located to the south of Church Island.

BIBLIOGRAPHY

Adams, Lincoln. "A Cremation Burial Site on Rattlesnake Island, Lake Winnipesaukee, West Alton, New Hampshire." *New Hampshire Archaeological Society Miscellaneous Papers*, 1968, 7–10. Personal papers of the treasurer of the New Hampshire Archaeological Society.

American Girl. "All Over the Map: Headline News in Girl Scouting." November 1950, 42.

Barre Daily Times. "Cyclone Hits Winnipesaukee: Damage Heavy." August 2, 1938, 3.

Batchellor, Albert Stillman. *State of New Hampshire Township Grants of Lands in New Hampshire Included in the Masonian Patent.* Concord, NH: Edward N. Pearson, January 1, 1896.

Beardsley, A.H. "Photography and the Summer Camp." *Photo-Era Magazine: The American Journal of Photography* (May 1926): 244–49.

Belknap County Registry of Deeds, 1841–present. Belknap County, New Hampshire, accessed 2023. https://www.nhdeeds.org//belknap-home.

Belknap, Jeremy. *The History of New Hampshire.* Dover, NH: O. Crosby and J. Varney, 1812.

Blaisdell, Paul H. *Three Centuries on Winnipesaukee.* Concord, NH: Paul H. Blaisdell, 1936.

Boston and Maine Corporation. "Winnipesaukee and About There: Description of the Lakes Region of Central New Hampshire, Boston and Maine Railroad Passenger Department." Boston: Boston and Maine Corporation, June 26, 1886.

Boston Evening Transcript. "Rattlesnake Island Lumbering." December 23, 1910, 1.

Boston Globe. "Awards $11,363.53 to Boston Woman." October 17, 1922, 8.

———. "Homing Pigeons on 100-Mile Flight." October 19, 1931, 10.

———. "Miss Brodeaur Denies Having Taken William P. Hales Papers." Deccember 20, 1920, 14.

———. "Obituary—Hobbs." April 15, 1996, 18.

———. "On Rattlesnake Island." December 24, 1910, 6.

———. "Trained Hawk Vanishes on Performance Before Expert." March 29, 1928, 7.

———. "$12,000 Loss on Rattlesnake Island." July 16, 1886, 3.

———. "Wells Buys 202 of the Islands." February 18, 1913, 32.

Boston Post. "Says She Took His Letters." November 30, 1920, 11.

Bowles, Ella Shannon. *Let Me Show You New Hampshire.* New York: Alfred A. Knopf, 1938.

Brewer, Ford. Sleeper Island Association Meeting Minutes.

Carroll County Registry of Deeds, 1840–present. Carroll County, New Hampshire, accessed 2023. https://www.carrollcountynhdeeds.gov.

Concord Monitor. "Music Festival Group Makes Plans for 1954." September 12, 1953, 6.

Crocker, William P. *Calverts Map of the Lake Region in New Hampshire, USA.* Weirs, NH: M.H. Calvert & Company, 1896.

Daily Item. "At Waveland." July 11, 1905, 8.

———. "Wavelandites Join the I'm Worried Club." February 5, 1912, 14.

Dunbar, Edith Flanders. *The Flanders Family from Europe to America.* Rutland, VT: Tuttle Publishing Company, 1935.

Dwight, Timothy. *Travels in New England and New York.* Cambridge, MA: Harvard University Press, 1969.

Fisher, Albert. *A Brief History of Alton Corners (1765–1810).* Alton, New Hampshire, 1973.

Fisher, Albert V., III. *The History of Alton New Hampshire Book I (1770–1800).* Alton, New Hampshire, 1979.

Fitchburg Sentinel. "Boston Arena Site of Coming Sportsman Show." January 6, 1944, 8.

Girl Scouts Inc. *Girl Scout Handbook.* New York: Girl Scouts Inc., 1929.

Goldthwait, Richard P. *Surficial Geology of the Wolfeboro–Winnipesaukee Area, New Hampshire.* Concord: State of New Hampshire Department of Resources and Economic Development, 1968.

Granite Monthly: A New Hamsphire Magazine. "Capt. Winborn Adams Sanborn." (November 1889): 287–90.

———, no. 389. "An Historic Event: Wolfeboro Celebrated Its One-Hundrenth and Fifieth Anniversary" (1920).

Griffin, Barton McLain. *The History of Alton.* Alton: Town of Alton, New Hampshire, 1960.

———. *The History of Alton: A Portrait in Granite.* Somersworth: New Hampshire Publishing Company, 1965.

Hale, Judson. "The Six States." *Inside New England,* no. 254 (1982).

Hamilton, Susan. "The Early Years." Chapter 2 in *Hit Woman: Adventures in Life and Love During the Golden Age of Pulp Music: A Memoir.* Wolfeboro, NH: Hitwoman Publishing, 2013.

Hammond, Otis Grant. "The Mason Title and Its Relations to New Hampshire and Massachusetts." In *The Mason Title.* Worcester, MA: American Antiquinarian Society, October 1916.

Heald, Bruce D., PhD. *A History of the New Hampshire Abenaki.* Charleston, SC: The History Press, 2014.

Hurd, D. Hamilton. *History of Merrimack and Belknap Counties, New Hampshire.* Philadelphia, PA: J.W. Lewis and Company, 1885.

Kriegsman, Alan M. "Lessons Learned: Students and Their Teachers." *Washington Post,* August 21, 1977.

Mathews, Allan. *Lake Winnipesaukee: Town Settlements and History: Including the Towns of Laconia, Center Harbor, Moultonborough, Wolfeboro, Alton, Meredith, Gilford and Tuftonboro.* Rockland, ME: Picton Press, 2009.

Modell, David. "Ring Dike Complex of the Belknap Mountains, New Hampshire." Geological Society of America, 1936.

Musical Currier. "New Hampshire Holds Festival." October 15, 1953, 23.

New Hampshire Bicententary Scrapbook. Durham, NH, 1813–23.

New York Times. "Hedy Spielters Recital: American Pianist Makes a Favorable Impression at Barbizon." March 17, 1930, 19.

———. "Jules Epailly, Ex-Actor, Dead; Known Also as Piano Teacher." May 2, 1967, 47.

———. "Verdict Is Set Aside in $75,000 Ship Suit." January 8, 1931, 6.

Parker, Benjamin Franklin. *History of Wolfeborough.* Cambridge, MA: Press of Caustic and Claflin, 1901.

Piotrowski, Thaddeus. *The Indian Heritage of New Hampshire and Northern New England.* Jefferson, NC: McFarland & Company Inc., 2002.

Portsmouth Herald. "Birds Eye Views." January 26, 1910, 4.

————. "N.H. Boasts Newest City in U.S. Fisherville, on Ice, Incorporated." March 19, 1940, 1.

Rutland Daily Herald. "Buys 202 Islands: Brother of Rutland Woman Heads a Big Incorporated Company." March 16, 1912, 5.

Sneller, Joseph. "Summer Music Camps Show Growth in Recent Decades." *Musical America*, April 10, 1955, 29.

Terry, Virginia Sleeper. *Robert Sleeper, Sr. Family History—Epping New Hampshire to Warren Center, PA, with Accounts of the Sleeper Family Dating from Thomas Sleeper of Hampton, NH.* N.p.: V. Sleeper Terry, 1999.

Wallis, L. Theodore. "The New Sport of Aquaplanning." *Outing* (1914): 143–47.

INDEX

A

Alton 11, 12, 33, 56, 76, 95, 103, 117, 126

B

Baker Island. *See* Keniston Island
Barndoor Islands 32, 65, 103, 105, 110
Big Barndoor Island 103, 104
Birch Island 75. *See also* Treasure Island
Blueberry Island 117, 130
Browns Island. *See* Melody Island

C

Camp Mishe Mokwa 77
Canney's Island. *See* Woodman's Cove Island

C

Chip Island 131
Church Island 125, 126, 132, 133
Coffin Island. *See* Grant Island
Cub Island 75

D

Diamond Island 15, 31, 56, 65, 103
Diamond Island House 66
Dr. Smith Island. *See* Littlest Mud Island

F

Fisher Island. *See* Grant Island
Flanders Island 34. *See also* Sleepers Island
Fox, William 108, 112, 128

G

Gate Island 117, 132
Gilford 12, 17, 37, 100
Grant Island 127

H

Hale, William Pillsbury 41
Half-Mile Island. *See* Plum Island
Harbour Island 132
Harmony Island 117, 120
Haven, Nathaniel Appleton 36, 56, 65

J

Jib Island 133

K

Keel Island 117, 133
Keniston Island 119, 130, 132

L

Libby, Henry Forrest 58, 113
Little Keniston II Island 117
Little Keniston I Island 117
Little Mark Island 97, 99
Littlest Mud Island 108, 126
Lone Pine Island 132

M

Melody Island 112, 119, 120, 121, 122, 123, 124, 125, 130, 131, 132, 133
Melody Island School of Music 123
Moose Island 95
Mount Major Island 99
Mud Island. *See* Melody Island
Mystery Island. *See* Quarter-Mile Island

O

Overnight Island 117, 132

P

Perkins, Harry 95, 105, 107
Plum Island 101

Q

Quarter-Mile Island 101

R

Rattlesnake Island 15, 16, 18, 24, 31, 32, 33, 38, 39, 40, 55, 56, 57, 58, 59, 61, 62, 63, 65, 75, 90, 95, 103, 111, 115, 128
Redhead Island. *See* Treasure Island

Roberts, Sewall 101, 104
Rogers, David C. 121, 128
Rogers, Nathaniel 56, 58, 115

S

Sanders, George 37, 75, 118
Scavenger Island 117, 132
Shelter Island 117, 132
Ship Island 31, 90, 95, 96
Sleeper, Nehemiah 11, 37
Sleepers Island 11, 15, 19, 31, 32,
        33, 34, 38, 40, 46, 48, 50, 52,
        57, 63, 65, 75, 86, 93, 127
Spider Island 126, 131, 132, 133
Spooner, Frederick Carroll 68

T

Treasure Island 75–93

U

Upper Shoe Island 131

V

Varney Island No. 1. *See* Melody
        Island
Varney Island No. 2. *See* Littlest
        Mud Island
Varney Islands 12, 17, 31, 52, 119
Varney, Joseph 103, 117, 121
Visibility Laboratory 70

W

Waveland Island. *See* Keniston
        Island
Wentworth, Mark Hunting 28, 56
Winch Island 117, 130, 131, 132,
        133
Wolfeboro 12, 15, 24, 28, 100, 103,
        104, 108, 111, 115, 117
Woodman's Cove Island 99
Worcester Island 115, 117, 127

ABOUT THE AUTHOR

Stephanie Erickson is a former geologist turned high school science educator. Stephanie has a Bachelor of Science degree in geology from the University of New Hampshire and a Master of Education in Digital Technology Integration degree from Southern New Hampshire University. She currently lives in southern New Hampshire with her husband, Tim. Stephanie is an avid researcher and sailor and a self-professed science geek. Stephanie, her husband and their black Lab, Obsidian ("Sid"), love visiting national parks, making maple syrup in their sugar shack, Black Dog Sugar, and enjoy their island camp, Labrador Retreat, on Sleepers Island in Lake Winnipesaukee. Stephanie resides in New Boston, New Hampshire, with her family.

Visit us at
www.historypress.com